The Girls' Guide to Life

by Catherine Dee

WITH ILLUSTRATIONS BY ALI DOUGLASS

LITTLE, BROWN AND COMPANY
New York ❧ Boston

ALSO BY CATHERINE DEE:

The Girls' Book of Friendship
The Girls' Book of Love
The Girls' Book of Success
The Girls' Book of Wisdom

**To my happening niece, Jessie Langer,
and America's current generation of girls, plus all
the parents, teachers, counselors, and mentors
committed to their success**

Little, Brown and Company

Time Warner Book Group
1271 Avenue of the Americas, New York, NY 10020
Visit our Web site at www.lb-teens.com

Second Edition: August 2005

Acknowledgments of permission to reprint previously published material
appear on pages 138–139.

Library of Congress Cataloging-in-Publication Data

Dee, Catherine.
The girls' guide to life / by Catherine Dee ; with
illustrations by Ali Douglass.—2nd ed.
p. cm.
Includes bibliographical references (p.) and index.
ISBN 0-316-73628-7
1. Girls—United States—Juvenile literature. 2. Teenage girls—United States—Juvenile
literature. 3. Sex role—United States—Juvenile literature. 4. Sexism—United States—
Juvenile literature. 5. Women's rights—United States—Juvenile literature. 6.
Feminism—United States—Juvenile literature. I. Douglass, Ali, ill.
II. Title.
HQ798.D397 2005
305.23'082—dc22

2004023274

10 9 8 7 6 5 4 3 2 1

Q-DB

Printed in the United States of America

The text was set in 11 pt. Diotima Roman, and the display typefaces are Ad Lib, Fontesque,
Khaki Two, and American Typewriter

Thanks!

This book was created thanks to the support and enthusiasm of many exceptional people:

★ Megan Tingley, vice president at Little, Brown, who was my editor for the first edition; Mary Gruetzke, my editor since 2000, and Amy Hsu, my current editor, plus book designer Julie Schroeder and the rest of the team at Little, Brown

★ Jonathan Ganz, my fabulous feminist husband

★ Fran Zeiner, my awesome mom, who gave me a copy of Marlo Thomas's girl-affirming book *Free to Be . . . You & Me* when I was six; Orson Dee, my superb dad, and my other great family members Dick, Hal, Vicky, Sarah, Ryan, Charley, Mike, Jeremy, Jessie, Jack, and Ben

★ Sara Mancini of Girls Incorporated of the Island City and Elizabeth Carlassare, who offered lots of insightful feedback on the manuscript

★ Everyone who provided a personal story or allowed me to reprint material

★ The many people and organizations who directly or indirectly helped me make this edition factually correct, relevant, and up-to-date, including Nancy Gruver and Joe Kelly of New Moon Publishing and Dads & Daughters, Caroline Ticarro-Parker of Mind on the Media, Jean Kilbourne, the Guerrilla Girls, Gloria Steinem, Robin Morgan, Amy Richards and Marianne Schnall of Feminist.com, Girls Incorporated, the Girl Scouts, the National Organization for Women (NOW), the Feminist Majority Foundation, *Ms.* magazine and the Ms. Foundation, the American Association of University Women (AAUW), Daughters, the Girls, Women + Media project, the White House Project, the Women's Sports Foundation, the National Coalition of Girls' Schools, Independent Means, Catalyst, the Center for the American Woman and Politics, Business and Professional Women USA, the Third Wave Foundation, Teen Voices, the Anorexia Bulimia Net, American Demographics, Gender PAC, GenderGap.com, Girl Power!, Girls Matter, Girls' Pipeline to Power, Google, Media Watch, the Melpomene Institute, Model Mugging, *More*, the National Association of Anorexia Nervosa and Associated Disorders, the National Center for Victims of Crime, the National Coalition for Women and Girls in Education, the National Eating Disorders Association, the National Women's Law Center, the NOW Legal Defense and Education Fund, Outward Bound, Teen Health and the Media, the U.S. Department of Education, and the Women's Bureau of the U.S. Department of Labor

Contents

Your Personal Life

At School

Introduction

Hello and welcome to *The Girls' Guide to Life*!

Do you ever find yourself:

★ Noticing how TV commercials are filled with flawlessly gorgeous women, and feeling insecure about how you look by comparison?

★ Keeping your thoughts to yourself in case someone won't like you if you're opinionated?

★ Wondering why so many magazine articles are about putting on makeup and selecting the best shampoo?

★ Raising your hand in class—only to have the teacher call on the loud guy next to you?

★ Wondering why, in the twenty-first century, we *still* haven't had a female president?

★ Getting stuck doing more housework than your brother?

★ Feeling annoyed by guys whistling at you or making obnoxious comments?

★ Being awesome in a coed sport but getting left out of the action?

If you answered yes to any of these questions, this book is for you. It's meant to help you get the most out of being a girl in America right now and successfully deal with any sexism you may face.

What's in this book? Background information on fifteen key issues, plus things you can do, both in your own life and as an activist, true stories from a wide variety of people about their personal experiences, historical "firsts," interesting facts and figures, cool quotes, quizzes, work sheets, and recommended books, magazines, and Web sites to explore.

I wrote *The Girls' Guide to Life* because when I was a growing up, I needed a book like it. When I was playing coed soccer in ninth-grade P.E., I could run just as fast as the boys on my team and was often open to receive the ball, but the guys didn't utilize my talent by passing to me. I could have scored plenty of goals for my team if only I'd been entrusted with the ball.

In addition, I didn't have an "hourglass" figure like the women I saw on TV and in magazines. I was flat-chested and lacking in hips, which made me feel insecure. And while I knew I was pretty smart and had good ideas, I was reluctant to express myself too much for fear of what people would think of a direct, outspoken girl.

If I'd understood then some of the things I do now—like the fact that boys may ignore girls in P.E. because they're afraid good female athletes will make them look bad, that 95 percent of females on the planet don't look like the other five percent who are model material, and that girls are subtly rewarded for keeping quiet—I might have had a better time and handled myself better as a teen.

So here you have it—all the information I can impart to you about growing up female and handling sexism, should you encounter it. Thanks to women's rights activists, life for girls has improved since I was growing up, and it's gotten better still since the first edition of this book was published in 1997. Most adults are now hyper-aware of the challenges girls face, and there've been considerable efforts toward helping girls succeed. In many ways, these efforts have worked. For example, boys used to outperform girls academically, but now it's girls who are doing better overall. And girls are generally more self-confident now than they used to be. This book celebrates that kind of progress.

On the other hand, as U.S. Supreme Court Justice Sandra Day O'Connor says, "Despite the encouraging and wonderful gains and the changes for women which have occurred in my lifetime, there is still room to advance and to promote correction of the remaining deficiencies and imbalances." It's possible you'll have to deal with at least some of the issues discussed in this book, either now, in the next few years, or in your twenties.

Regardless of what you experience, you'll be ahead just by being informed. The more you understand about how sexism can affect you, the better prepared you'll be to handle it. And once you've increased your awareness, you can use this knowledge to make the world better for all of femalekind.

So the next time you're in a situation where you feel that something isn't fair to you or to girls and women in general, don't despair. As they say, knowledge is power. When you understand what's going on and you know your options, you can make informed, self-respecting decisions. As you do this, you'll increase your odds of attaining personal happiness and success. And in the process, you'll help build respect for girls and women everywhere.

Happy reading!

 Nothing in life is to be feared, it is only to be understood.

—MARIE CURIE, physicist, chemist

A Quick Quiz: Women's Issues

DEFINING TERMS

1. What is the women's movement?
   a. An all-female group of immigrants making its way to the United States
   b. A new kind of belly dance
   c. The quest to achieve equality for women and girls

2. What is a feminist?
   a. Someone who supports the same economic, political, and social rights for everybody
   b. Someone who wants women to take over the earth
   c. A woman who wears a lot of frilly clothes and makeup

3. What is sexism?
   a. When girls wish they had the advantages boys have
   b. Favoring one age group
   c. Favoring boys or girls

4. Which of these is an example of sexism?
   a. A guy doing the dishes
   b. A teacher calling on only boys in class
   c. An elephant painting a picture

5. What does ERA stand for?
   a. Eat Red Apples
   b. End Racism Altogether
   c. Equal Rights Amendment

6. Which of these is an example of sexual harassment?
   a. Having someone snap your bra strap
   b. Being told by your parents that you can't date 'til you're fifteen
   c. Being told someone has a crush on you

7. Which of these is a stereotype?
   a. Only females can bear children
   b. Many girls grow up to become scientists
   c. Guys are better than girls in science

LIFE IN AMERICA

8. Women generally make less ____ than men.
   a. Money
   b. Cake
   c. Time for their families

9. When a woman gets married, it's traditional that she:
   a. Wear a short red dress
   b. Walk down the aisle by herself
   c. Give up her her last name and take her husband's

10. What percentage of women ages 18–24 call themselves feminists?
    a. 1
    b. 25
    c. 56

11. As of 2005, women made up _____ percent of U.S. Congressional Representatives.
    a. 31
    b. 15
    c. 105

12. When did the modern American women's movement formally start?
    a. When the men's movement ended
    b. When Susan B. Anthony's brothers left the toilet seat up and Susan fell in
    c. When women won the right to vote in 1920

ANSWERS

1. c. The goal is liberty and justice for all women and girls.
2. a. Some people believe it's a person who dislikes men and wants to take away their power, but this is incorrect. A feminist is simply a person of either gender who believes in equality for both.
3. c. Also referred to as *gender bias*, it's most commonly directed at girls and women.
4. b.
5. c. This proposed constitutional amendment would prohibit discrimination on the basis of gender. Although it was introduced years ago, it still hasn't been approved.
6. a. Sexual harassment is any type of unwanted sexually oriented comments or touching.
7. c. A stereotype is a generally believed idea that isn't always true. When it comes to science, boys don't have a genetic advantage; girls can do just as well.
8. a. According to the Bureau of Labor Statistics, on average, women earn less money—only 77.5 cents for each dollar men earn.
9. c. The tradition of women changing their names originally reflected symbolic "ownership" by their husbands. Wives are no longer seen as a form of property, but the name-change tradition has stuck.
10. c. 56 percent, according to a 2003 Harris poll. This is an increase of 5 percent over 1995 figures. But when it comes to actual *support* for feminism (regardless of who embraces the term *feminist*, the data is even more positive: 92 percent of 18-to-24-year-old women rate the women's movement favorably.
11. b. 15 percent of Congress was female in 2005.
12. c. The women's movement started decades earlier, but this landmark achievement got the spotlight.

Timeline: Exciting Moments in Women's History

In some of the world's earlier societies, females were highly respected, and the contributions of both men and women were valued, which made for high productivity. Unfortunately, the balance was upset by a collective male force determined to dominate, and this set into motion events (such as the Salem Witch Trials in 1692) that "put women in their place." When America was founded, women were literally second-class citizens—they couldn't vote or own property, and they faced many forms of discrimination.

Since then, women have steadily worked toward achieving equal rights. In the 1900s, they began making progress, and in the 1960s, they started making real headway. Here are some milestones since the mid-1800s:

1848: A meeting called the Seneca Falls Women's Rights Convention was held in New York State to discuss the need for women's equality.

1872: Victoria Woodhull formed her own political party and became the first woman to run for president (she lost to Ulysses S. Grant).

1910: The first International (Working) Women's Day was celebrated on March 8, commemorating an 1857 demonstration advocating for better working conditions for female garment and textile workers.

1916: Jeannette Rankin, a Republican from Montana, was the first woman elected to the U.S. House of Representatives.

1920: After a long struggle that began in the mid-1800s, American women won the right to vote with the ratification of the Nineteenth Amendment to the Constitution.

1923: Alice Paul drafted the Equal Rights Amendment (ERA), a constitutional amendment stating that women must be treated equally.

1942: While men were off fighting World War II, women were paid well to work in factories. The term "Rosie the Riveter" was coined to reflect this role.

1963: Women lobbied for equal opportunities at work, and Congress passed the Equal Pay Act, which was intended to guarantee women in similar jobs as men the same earning power.

In a bestselling book called *The Feminine Mystique*, Betty Friedan made the case that women need more than marriage and kids to be happy.

1966: The National Organization for Women (NOW), the most prominent women's rights activist group, was founded.

1968: The first major demonstration for women's rights took place at the Miss America Pageant, when "women's liberation" groups formed as the female arm of a mostly male student activism movement.

The first national Women's Liberation Conference helped women from thirty-seven states and Canada organize their plan of action.

1970: On the fiftieth anniversary of the ratification of the Nineteenth Amendment, more than one hundred thousand women participated in demonstrations.

1971: The National Women's Political Caucus was founded to work toward equal representation for women at all levels of the political system. Today it has considerable influence, distributing hundreds of thousands of dollars to the campaigns of women running for office.

1972: *Ms.* magazine's first issue was published with Gloria Steinem, the most well-known leader of the women's movement, as editor.

The ERA was passed by the Senate and sent to the states to be ratified. Too few states ratified it, so it failed to become a law (and again failed in 1982).

1973: The Supreme Court's ruling in the case of Roe v. Wade upheld women's right to privacy as including the right to have first-trimester abortions in all states. Feminists hailed the ruling because it ensured that women have control over their own bodies.

1975: Title IX, a law that banned sex discrimination in college sports and increased athletic opportunities for girls and women, was passed.

1977: Janet Guthrie became the first female race-car driver to compete in the famous Indianapolis 500.

1979: The Supreme Court ruled in support of company policies that favor the hiring and promotion of women and minorities.

1980: For the first time since the passage of the Nineteenth Amendment, women as a group voted significantly differently from men for president (more men voted for Ronald Reagan than women). This phenomenon was named the "gender gap."

1981: Sandra Day O'Connor was the first woman appointed to the Supreme Court.

1983: TV newscaster Christine Craft was fired for being "too unattractive, too old, and not deferential enough to men." She filed a lawsuit and won.

Sally Ride became the first female astronaut, serving as mission specialist on the space shuttle *Challenger*'s second voyage.

A landmark case of wage discrimination in Washington state was resolved in favor of women who weren't earning as much as men in comparable (similar) jobs.

1984: Walter Mondale made history as the first major-party presidential candidate to choose a female running mate, Geraldine Ferraro.

1985: EMILY's (Early Money Is Like Yeast) List, an organization created to help Democratic, pro-choice women candidates pay for their election campaigns, was founded.

1987: The Supreme Court ruled that male-only clubs unfairly discriminate against women. The Rotary, Lions, and Kiwanis Clubs opened their doors to women.

The Feminist Majority Foundation, a research- and action-focused group dedicated to women's equality, was founded.

1992: A bestselling book called *Backlash: The War Against American Women*, by Susan Faludi, documented how sexism was still going strong in America and certain groups were making a concerted effort to erode its gains.

Professor Anita Hill testified before an all-male committee that Supreme Court nominee Clarence Thomas sexually harassed her. He was confirmed anyway, but her testimony made sexual harassment a mainstream issue.

Women made up 54 percent of all registered voters (10 million more women voted than men). A record number of women ran for office and were elected (forty-seven in the House of Representatives and six in the Senate). Carol Moseley Braun of Illinois became the first African-American female senator. All of this made 1992 "The Year of the Woman."

Congress passed the Family Leave Act, which mandated that companies treat women and men the same way (for example, it allowed fathers to take time off to care for their newborn babies).

1993: "Take Our Daughters to Work Day" was established by the Ms. Foundation as an annual girl-empowering event.

1995: The Supreme Court ruled that public military schools can't discriminate against women, allowing Shannon Faulkner to become the first female cadet at the previously all-male Citadel.

1996: Women won nineteen of America's forty-four gold medals and women's Olympic events were prominently featured in TV coverage.

As a result of the largest-ever gender gap, Bill Clinton was re-elected president.

1997: The Women's National Basketball Association was founded. Attendance at games rivaled that of various men's sports.

The Lilith Fair, an all-female music festival, received rave reviews and consistently sold out.

1998: Eileen Collins became America's first female space shuttle commander.

1999: Three cheers: In New Hampshire, women held three major state offices at the same time: governor (Jeanne Shaheen), Senate president (Beverly Hollingsworth), and House speaker (Donna Sytek).

2000: Women were 42 percent of the athletes competing in the Sydney Olympics. They were permitted to compete in formerly all-male sports, including pole vaulting and weightlifting.

Hillary Clinton became the first first lady elected to the United States Senate.

2002: Nancy Pelosi was elected U.S. House minority leader, making her the first woman to lead either party in Congress.

2003: Opponents of Title IX attempted to do away with it. However, the 30-year-old law, which increased female participation in high school sports by more than 800 percent since its debut, was reaffirmed.

Annika Sörenstam became the first woman to compete in a men's golf tournament in 58 years.

Take Our Daughters to Work Day, now an event with millions of participants, became Take Our Daughters and Sons to Work Day, in part "to broaden the discussion about the competing challenges of work and family."

2004: The largest pro-choice march ever (more than 1 million people) took place in Washington, D.C.

For more information:

33 Things Every Girl Should Know About Women's History, edited by Tonya Bolden (Crown, 2002). Covers everything from how women won the vote to how they've progressed in athletics.

Your Personal Life

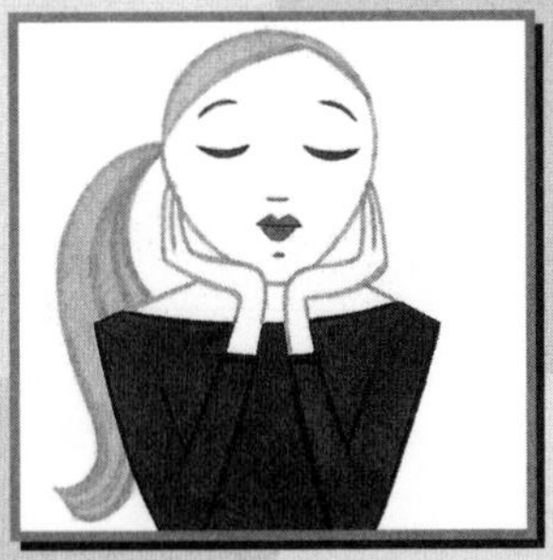

Chapter 1

Looking Out for #1

Who's the most confident person you know—the one who most strongly believes in herself and who's least afraid to say what's on her mind?

She undoubtedly has high self-esteem, which, according to *Webster's* dictionary, means "confidence and satisfaction in oneself." Psychologist Nathaniel Branden further defines it as "confidence in our ability to think, learn, choose, and make appropriate decisions . . . and in our right to be happy; confidence that achievement, success, friendship, respect, love, and fulfillment are appropriate to us."

Your self-esteem is vitally important because it has a "ripple effect." Your self-confidence level colors how you feel about yourself, which dictates how you behave. Your behavior affects how people respond to you. For example, let's say you're feeling insecure and you put yourself down to a friend. This could make her start thinking less highly of you and perhaps not treating you as well as a friend should. This behavior, in turn, could make you feel bad about yourself and start the cycle again.

This book devotes a whole chapter to self-esteem because you'll need it in large quantities if you're going to stand up for your rights and the rights of all girls and women. In order to stand up for yourself, you have to believe deep down that *you deserve those rights* and you're worthy of them (yes, you most definitely are!).

How Do Girls Rate on Self-Esteem?

In the 1990s, some studies found that girls have lower self-esteem than boys, and that it gets worse as they reach adolescence and go through high school. Since then, other research has shown better results, and some studies say the situation is now exactly the opposite. A 2003 Greenfield Online survey of girls ages 7 to 14 found that 75 percent of girls like themselves just the way the are, and research at the University of Wisconsin concluded that girls have only slightly lower levels of self-esteem than boys.

On the other hand, girls are still scoring major points for keeping quiet, behaving well, and looking attractive, as opposed to being bold, expressing themselves, and accomplishing things, and this is not helpful for building confidence. And despite the rosier studies, some girls still don't feel as self-assured as they'd like. Some worry excessively about what people think of them. Fearing that classmates won't like them if they express strong opinions, many girls keep their thoughts to themselves. Others try not to seem "too smart" since some boys feel threatened by intelligent girls. "If a teacher asks a question, I'll often know the answer but I won't raise my hand because it would make me look like a nerd," says Sydney Bird, a seventh-grader in Berkeley, California. "Sometimes I do speak up without realizing it, but then I wonder whether I should have."

The Trouble with Dumbing Yourself Down

If you've been a quiet person all your life, then it's a natural state for you; if you haven't, it's probably not, and you are, in effect, masking your true self. This could cause problems for you later. For example, when you graduate from high school, you may continue being quiet but find that college professors and potential employers expect you to project more outward confidence and regularly voice ideas. Or you may find that you have trouble in relationships because you don't ask for what you want. Or you may have a job that pays you less than you're worth, but you just can't get up the nerve to ask for a raise.

Self-esteem affects virtually everything you do and influences how successful you'll be in all areas of your life. If you get in the habit of nurturing your self-esteem and acting and sounding confident, you're sure to see a *positive* ripple effect.

THINGS TO DO ———————————

Determine Your Confidence Level

Is your esteem excellent? Here's a worksheet to assess where you stand. Make a copy of this page to fill out, or write your answers on a separate sheet of paper. Then score your responses with the key on the next page. If your rating could be higher, do this again next year to see if anything's changed.

PART 1

1. What are five positive things about you?

   _____

2. What would your friends say is your best quality?

   _____

3. What would your mother or father say is your best quality?

   _____

4. Name two things you're good at:

   _____

5. Name one thing you're proud of:

   _____

6. Name two things you like about your body:

   _____

PART 2

Put a *T* for true or an *F* for false in front of each statement.

___ When my teacher praises me, I believe her or him.
___ I usually say what I mean.
___ If someone disagrees with my opinion, I still believe what I believe.
___ I basically like the way I look.
___ I'm happy with myself the way I am.
___ If someone compliments me, I usually respond with "thank you."
___ I rarely put myself down in conversations with other kids.
___ I believe in my ability to make a contribution in the world.
___ If I have a goal, I give my all to accomplish it.
___ I believe people can change their attitudes.

WHAT YOUR ANSWERS MEAN

If you thought of positive answers to all the questions in Part 1, you genuinely like and respect yourself—a sign of high self-esteem. If you couldn't think of positive answers to all the questions, try to develop a better sense of your strengths.

For Part 2, count your "true" answers. Here's what your total means:

1-3 "true": You aren't very self-confident. Read the rest of this section for suggestions to improve your self-esteem.

4-6 "true": Your self-esteem is about average, but you can definitely improve it. See the next section for details.

7-10 "true": Congratulations, you have great self-esteem! Read the rest of this section for tips on keeping your self-esteem level up.

—adapted from *Developing Self-Esteem: A Positive Guide for Personal Success*, by Connie Palladino

Listen to Yourself Talk

What you say often reveals how you feel about yourself. How do you talk about you? Here are tip-offs that your self-esteem may be low, plus ways you can start sounding—and feeling—more confident.

★ Ending statements by raising your voice to a higher tone and saying ". . . you know?" This indicates that you need someone to approve of what you just said. It's better simply to finish what you're saying in the same normal tone of voice.

★ Putting yourself down with comments like "I hate my thighs" or "I'm no good at this." Put-downs have a way of implying that you're a bad person, when *you aren't*. You don't have to brag, and it's okay if you aren't perfect, but there's no need to harp on what you don't like about yourself.

★ Not accepting compliments. If someone says something nice about you, instead of disagreeing or downplaying the remark (such as with a sarcastic comment), just say "Thanks!" This might feel weird at first, but you'll get used to it.

★ Saying "I don't know," even if you clearly do know.

★ Agreeing with someone even if you don't really agree. You don't have to blurt out your opposing opinion, but you don't have to *agree*.

Speak Up!

The most fundamental thing you can do to improve your self-confidence is to talk. That's right! Not mindless babbling, just chiming in when it makes sense and putting your good ideas out there for the world to consider.

However, keep in mind that using your voice carries with it certain responsibilities. Some girls go overboard with self-expression, becoming loud and overbearing, which adds no more value than saying nothing. "Speaking up" doesn't mean bragging, ignoring others' feelings, or criticizing people. It's not monopolizing conversations or being rude. It's simply *being comfortable stating your point of view* and asking for what you want or deserve, if that's appropriate.

For example, one day, thirteen-year-old Ana Jeronimus of Duluth, Minnesota, wanted to play baseball with some boys on her street. When she told them she wanted to play, they said no. So she got her glove, then went and asked again.

"One kid in particular was being mean, as if I didn't belong there," she recalls. She didn't see any reason why she shouldn't play. Finally, the boys offered to let her be "full-time catcher." She declined and left again. When she came back, the mean boy had left and the others apologized and let her play. Ana says, "I was glad I spoke up for myself because they realized they'd done the wrong thing. I feel pretty confident about myself now."

To get inspired to stand up for yourself, think of all the successful women who gracefully speak their minds. If your mom or aunt is a good example, start with her. There's also Congresswoman Nancy Pelosi, Senator Hillary Clinton, National Security Advisor Condoleeza Rice, talk-show host Oprah Winfrey, comedian Janeane Garofalo, writer Maya Angelou, and musicians Ani DiFranco and the Dixie Chicks, to name just a few. Then practice saying what you think. The more you do it, the more natural it will feel!

Another idea is to attend an open mike event hosted by an organization called That Takes Ovaries, which is devoted to women's and girls' empowerment. Check its event schedule on *www.thattakesovaries.org* to see when one will be happening in your area.

Keep a Journal

Do you have a journal in which you can record events, feelings, ideas, and observations about the things that happen to you, as well as goals and dreams? Your journal can be as simple as a spiral notebook from the drugstore or as elaborate as a bound cloth book with beautiful pages and a cover you've decorated yourself. You don't have to write a lot or even record something every day; just think of it as a place where you can confidentially express yourself.

According to psychologist David D. Burns, author of *The Feeling Good Handbook*, when you put your thoughts down on paper, you develop perspective—you're able to stand back and view yourself more clearly. Clarifying your ideas in writing is helpful because when the opportunity arises to voice them, you'll feel more sure of yourself. You may also discover new morsels of knowledge about yourself by letting your brain "doodle"—writing whatever pops into your head. With journaling, "there's always a surprise, a revelation," says writer Gail Godwin. "During the act of writing, I have told myself something that I didn't know I knew."

Having trouble getting started? Try one of these low-pressure exercises:

★ Write about a conversation you had with someone during the day and how it affected you.

★ List the things you value most (for example, getting good grades, being honest, getting along with your parents), and explain why.

★ List ten things you dream of doing someday.

★ Set goals: What do you want to accomplish by the time you're fifteen, twenty, twenty-five?

★ Write a poem about yourself.

★ Cut out images from magazines and make a collage about yourself.

For a little perspective on journaling, read famous girls' diaries. Here are some good ones:

Anne Frank: The Diary of a Young Girl, by Anne Frank, translated by B. M. Mooyaart (Prentice Hall, 1993)

Girls: A History of Growing Up Female in America, by Penny Colman (Scholastic, 2000); includes a variety of girls' journal entries.

Only Opal: The Diary of a Young Girl, by Opal Whiteley, adapted by Jane Boulton (Putnam, 1994)

Zlata's Diary: A Child's Life in Sarajevo, by Zlata Filipovic (Penguin, 1994)

You can also read books *about* journal keeping, including *The Freedom Writers Diary: How a Teacher and 150 Teens Used Writing to Change Themselves and the World Around Them*, by the Freedom Writers with Erin Gruwell (Doubleday, 1999).

Find a Mentor

Is there a woman (other than a family member) in your life—such as a teacher or coach—who has your best interests at heart? She could be your mentor. According to the National Mentoring Partnership, mentors are "good listeners, people who care, people who want to help young people bring out strengths that are already there."

If you're lucky enough to already have a mentor, let this person know how much you appreciate her support, which will make her want to continue guiding and inspiring you. If you don't have a mentor, you can probably get one. Where? Big Brothers/Big Sisters, an organization that pairs kids ages six to seventeen with adult volunteers. With your big sister you might go to a movie or arts event, or you might just sit in the park and talk. For contact information, look on the Web at www.bbbsa.com or in the white pages under *Big Brothers/Big Sisters*, or contact the organization directly at 230 North 13th Street, Philadelphia, PA 19107; (215) 567-7000. You can also find other mentoring organizations on the National Mentoring Center Web site, www.nwrel.org/mentoring/organizations.html.

Join a Girls' Organization

Many girls say that being in an organization such as the Girl Scouts or Girls Inc. boosts their confidence. These organizations focus on developing your leadership abilities, and they let you practice planning, organizing, speaking, being creative, and lots more. Projects vary according to each local chapter but generally include such activities as organizing beach cleanups and conferences, building bridges, and painting group houses for runaway kids. To find a nearby Girl Scouts council, visit www.girlscouts.org; to find a local Girls Incorporated center, visit www.girlsinc.com.

Explore New Interests, Develop New Passions

What do you do after or outside of school? Skill-building activities such as debate, public speaking, martial arts, acting, and playing a musical instrument are excellent ways to develop your self-confidence. Try a variety of things and you'll probably gravitate toward one or two that you want to pursue more seriously. Your chosen pursuits become part of your self-concept and bring new dimension to your life, which can't help but make you feel good about who you are. (If any of your activities are team sports, that's especially cool; Chapter 9, Know the Score, tells why.)

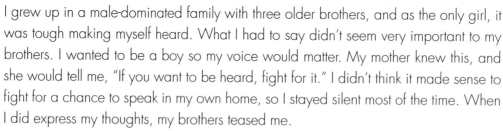

Finding Your Voice

By BROOKE HODESS ★ Boston, Massachusetts

I grew up in a male-dominated family with three older brothers, and as the only girl, it was tough making myself heard. What I had to say didn't seem very important to my brothers. I wanted to be a boy so my voice would matter. My mother knew this, and she would tell me, "If you want to be heard, fight for it." I didn't think it made sense to fight for a chance to speak in my own home, so I stayed silent most of the time. When I did express my thoughts, my brothers teased me.

However, all this changed when I went to Wheaton—an all-women's college at the time—where I developed a strong sense of self-esteem. The message was: Believe in yourself, value your strengths, nurture your drive. I had an array of strong, outspoken female role models—not just professors, administrators, and the president, but students as well. All the student leadership roles were filled by women. I developed a sense of belonging and an activist spirit. I started to believe in myself. I began to realize that I stood for things I was willing to fight for, and I began to find my voice.

Low self-esteem made me keep quiet at the dinner table when I was growing up, but now I've made up for that. If I had known then what I know now—that my voice would have mattered if I'd had faith in it—I might have spoken up more. And so I say to you: It's okay to speak up, to be outgoing, to know that you *are* important. Seek guidance from people who believe in you. Always remember who you are and where you've come from. And more than anything else, don't let anyone deny you your right to be heard.

LOOKING OUT FOR #1 —— 9

Phenomenal Woman

Pretty women wonder where my secret lies.
I'm not cute or built to suit a fashion model's
     size
But when I start to tell them,
They think I'm telling lies.
I say,
It's in the reach of my arms,
The span of my hips,
The stride of my step,
The curl of my lips.
I'm a woman
Phenomenally.
Phenomenal woman,
That's me.

I walk into a room
Just as cool as you please,
And to a man,
The fellows stand or
Fall down on their knees.
Then they swarm around me,
A hive of honey bees.
I say,
It's the fire in my eyes,
And the flash of my teeth,
The swing in my waist,
And the joy in my feet.
I'm a woman
Phenomenally.
Phenomenal woman,
That's me.

Men themselves have wondered
What they see in me.

They try so much
But they can't touch
My inner mystery.
When I try to show them
They say they still can't see.
I say,
It's in the arch of my back,
The sun of my smile,
The ride of my breasts,
The grace of my style.
I'm a woman

Phenomenally.
Phenomenal woman,
That's me.

Now you understand
Just why my head's not bowed.
I don't shout or jump about
Or have to talk real loud.
When you see me passing
It ought to make you proud.
I say,
It's in the click of my heels,
The bend of my hair,
The palm of my hand,
The need for my care.
'Cause I'm a woman
Phenomenally.
Phenomenal woman,
That's me.

—MAYA ANGELOU,
 poet, writer

Cool Quote

All serious daring starts from within.

—EUDORA WELTY, writer

FOR MORE INFORMATION

California Department of Education, Publication Sales, P.O. Box 271, Sacramento, CA 95812-0271, 800-995-4099; 916-445-1260; www.cde.ca.gov/cdepress/catalog/topics.html. Has self-esteem-oriented publications *Mariposa* for Latina girls and *Images* for African-American girls.

The Girls' Book of Success and *The Girls' Book of Wisdom*, edited by Catherine Dee (Little, Brown, 2003, 1999). Inspirational true stories, quotes, and fun facts.

GirlWise, by Julia DeVillers (Prima, 2002). The definitive guide to feeling "confident, capable, cool, and in control."

The Greatness of Girls, by Susan Strong (Andrews McMeel, 2001). Stories of how famous women faced and overcame obstacles while growing up.

Life is a Movie Starring You, by Jennifur Brandt (Warner, 2000). A well-written go-girl guide.

New Moon: The Magazine for Girls and Their Dreams, 34 E. Superior St. #200, Duluth MN 55802, 800-381-4743, *www.newmoon.org.* The magazine and Web site "for every girl who wants her voice heard and her dreams taken seriously."

Ophelia Speaks, by Sara Shandler (Harper Perennial, 1999). Girls' personal accounts of challenges that impacted their self-esteem.

Teen Voices, Women Express, Inc., P.O. Box 120-027, Boston, MA 02112-0027, 888-882-8336, and Teen Voices Online (*www.teenvoices.com*). The magazine for when you outgrow *New Moon.*

33 Things Every Girl Should Know, by Tonya Bolden (Crown, 1998). Great essays about "girl buildup" by prominent women.

Chapter 2

Go Figure

Are you satisfied with the way you look? If you could change some of your features, would you?

Most girls say no, they aren't satisfied, and yes, they would definitely change something, or several things. Girls feel that they have to look "perfect" in order to be popular or even just accepted. They're also very judgmental of each other. "The message is if you aren't beautiful, change yourself or be doomed to the life of a social outcast!" says Ashley Olauson, twelve, of Edina, Minnesota.

That pressure is caused by our model-worshipping culture and idealized images of women that seem to be everywhere—staring out from magazines, dancing around on TV, on magazine covers, and appearing to be larger than life on billboards. Most of these images show thin, light-skinned women with blonde hair, large breasts (often enhanced with silicone), small hips, and long legs. Seeing images like these on a daily basis can easily warp your sense of what's "normal" and make you feel inadequate by comparison. In a *People* magazine poll asking women if they were influenced by the unrealistically thin images of Hollywood women, 80 percent said that images of women on TV, in movies, and in magazines made them feel insecure about their bodies.

Even though many girls look fine the way they are, they go to great lengths to obliterate what they see as physical flaws and try to live up to society's narrowly defined standards of beauty. Many girls are currently on diets or they've tried dieting.

Some exercise excessively, while others resort to cosmetic surgery such as breast enhancement, liposuction, or a nose job. One of every five girls ages twelve to nineteen has an eating disorder (the two common ones are anorexia and bulimia). "Here are all these gorgeous girls who think they're fat and ugly," says eating disorders specialist and psychologist Dr. Dina Zeckhausen of Atlanta. "I see how beautiful they are, and they don't know it."

Beauty Secrets

If you're not entirely satisfied with your looks, take a step back from assessing your features and think about the nature of beauty. Despite what's in the American media, the concept of what's beautiful is extremely subjective—people in different parts of the world (and even in the same parts of the world) have different ideas about what makes a woman attractive. According to Elaine Hatfield and Susan Sprecher, authors of *Mirror, Mirror . . . The Importance of Looks in Everyday Life,* "People in different cultures do not even agree on which features are *important,* much less what is good-looking and what is not." This is especially true when it comes to weight. Centuries ago, when it was hard for people to get enough to eat, heavy people were considered attractive because they were obviously well off, while thin people were seen as malnourished and poor. Dieting was considered abnormal as recently as the 1900s. And even today, some cultures, such as one in Matsiegenka, Peru, don't subscribe to the belief that super-thin women are attractive. In addition, beauty ideals, like fashions, have fluctuated over time. For example, in the 1920s it was fashionable to have small hips, and in the 1950s larger hips and a more voluptuous look (like Marilyn Monroe's) were in style.

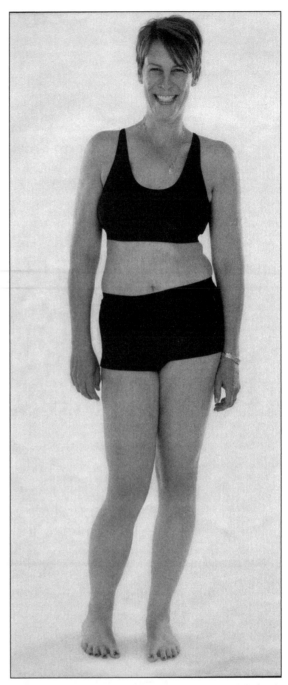

Actor and author Jamie Lee Curtis surprised and delighted women and girls everywhere when she appeared in *More* magazine as she *really* looks—with no makeup and no retouching—to help people see that celebrities aren't perfect, either. "There's a reality to the way I look without my clothes on," she says. "I don't have great thighs. I have very big breasts and a soft, fatty little tummy. And I've got back fat. People assume that I'm walking around in little spaghetti-strap dresses. It's insidious—glam Jamie, the perfect Jamie, the great figure, blah, blah, blah. It's such a fraud. And I'm the one perpetuating it."

Feel like you've gained some perspective? Now let's get back to how you feel about your looks. You probably don't love everything about your appearance, and that's fine—most people feel that way. It's fine to put effort into looking good by staying in shape, wearing clothes that flatter you, and putting on makeup, but try to keep your physical appearance in perspective. Focus on expressing the person you are and on doing the activities that bring you satisfaction. As author Susan Jane Gilman says in *Kiss My Tiara*, "Our gray matter has far better staying power than our thighs ever will; it has the capacity to endow us—and the world—with joy, enlightenment, and influence well into our old age. So why focus so much on shaping our bodies when we can shape history?" Incidentally, when you're not worrying about your body and you're actively engaged in your life, people will think you're *especially* beautiful!

THINGS TO DO

Learn the Media's Secrets

Did you know that the vast majority (95 percent) of girls and women don't look like models? Or that models are 9 percent taller and 23 percent thinner than the average woman? That's for starters. Then they're posed in ways that make them appear to be more attractive (such as more curvy) than they really are. But that's not the end. The photos are frequently airbrushed, retouched, and manipulated. For example, one woman's head may be used with another's body, and legs may be lengthened and made narrower (see Chapter 10, Selling Us Short, for more about images used in advertising). When all of this is finished, even *models* don't look like models: Cindy Crawford, for one, has confessed that she doesn't look like her supermodel image without all the makeup and styling.

Becoming aware of the differences between how people look in the real world and how they look in the world of media illusion is the first step to making peace with your feelings about your body. Look around at the girls and women walking down the street, at the mall, or anywhere. Every now and then you'll see someone who's conventionally beautiful, but for the most part, people look pretty average. Notice that they come in all shapes and sizes. Some are tall, some are short, some are overweight, some have athletic builds, some have darker skin, some have hair that's hard to tame, and some are older and graying. Remember that while media images may be engineered for perfection, the world is made up of the real girls and women you see everyday, each of whom is entirely unique—and uniquely attractive.

Discover Your Body's Talents and Strengths

A girl or woman using her body to accomplish something physical with energy and grace is a beautiful sight. Watching a soccer player kick a long goal is inspiring; so is the sight of a lanky marathon runner extending her lead on the pack, or a competitive swimmer churning up the water with a powerful butterfly stroke.

Hey, what can *your* body do? Develop your strength, flexibility, and physical agility through a sport such as dance, lifting weights, yoga, or karate (see Chapter 9, Know the Score, for more info on sports). Be proud of your amazing body and revel in its abilities!

Keep a Body Diary

You might feel that if you could change one thing about your looks, you'd suddenly feel supremely happy. It's possible, but it doesn't usually work that way; when one "defect" goes away, you're likely to find something else to criticize about yourself. Psychologists say the solution is not to change your body, since to a large extent genetics *can't* be changed (if you're stocky, constant aerobics won't make you thin). Instead, embrace your body as the highly functional and wonderful vessel you live in.

You can do this by keeping a body diary. Every night, write down whether you felt critical of your appearance during the day. Then ask yourself if there were other reasons you could have been upset (you may feel insecure about your body when you're reacting to unrelated events). If you determine that you were indeed upset about something else, write about it, and the negative body feelings may go away. End each diary entry by jotting down something you appreciate about your body or what it does for you.

Open Mouth, Insert . . . Food

You might be tempted to skip meals or cut carbs to lose weight, but this can backfire. For example, skipping breakfast can not only give you cravings later, it can negatively affect how you do in school. According to researchers at the University of Ulster in Northern Ireland, girls need a more satisfying breakfast than boys to perform at their best on tests. By contrast, boys do better on tests when they feel a little hungry. So don't forget: Healthy meals are necessary for a balanced diet.

Understand Eating Disorders

You've probably heard of anorexia and bulimia, the two unhealthy conditions that are especially common among teen girls (boys make up only 10 percent of those affected). With anorexia, a girl's weight falls below normal through dieting and excessive exercise. Bulimia is eating large amounts of food (bingeing), followed by getting rid of the food by vomiting or using laxatives (purging). These conditions disrupt your normal body functions and can put you in danger. For example, bulimia causes the production of excess stomach acids, which can damage your stomach lining. And the weight loss produced by anorexia can decrease muscle tone, cause osteoporosis, and, in some extreme cases, result in death. Gymnast Christy Henrich died from anorexia in 1994, and ballet dancer Heidi Guenther died in 1997 of problems suspected to be from an eating disorder.

Eating disorders are generally caused by psychological and emotional factors. If you have an eating disorder, you may be using food to comfort yourself or avoid unresolved feelings. You may adopt unhealthy eating patterns as a way of unconsciously controlling *something* if you feel that part of your life is out of control. Eating disorders can also be attempts to avoid some type of pressure (which could have originated in the past).

If you think you might have a problem with food, don't despair; it's treatable. However, it's *very* important that you talk to an adult you trust—such as a parent or your doctor—right away. To learn more about eating disorders, consult the resources on page 200.

Do you have a friend exhibiting symptoms of an eating disorder—for instance, she looks *way* too thin or she's surfing pro-anorexia Web sites? You can help. Don't criticize her, as this will only make her more anxious. Tell her that you're concerned, give her resources, and strongly suggest that she talk to someone who can help (and offer to go with her if she wants).

Turn Beauty Inside Out

The editors of *New Moon*, a cool magazine for girls, came up with an event called "Turn Beauty Inside Out" Day (TBIO, which takes place the third Wednesday in May, as an alternative to *People* magazine's appearance- and celebrity-focused "50 Most Beautiful People.") New Moon's "25 Beautiful Girls" are recognized for what they do and how it makes them beautiful. For a list of things you can do in the spirit of this event, go to the Mind on the Media Web site (www.motm.org). You can nominate a friend or sister (8–14 years old) for beautiful girl by writing to *New Moon*; for details, visit www.newmoon.org.

Compare Styles Across the Decades

See for yourself how the definition of beauty has changed through history. Get a friend and go to the library for a little research project. Gather magazines or books from two separate decades that are at least one decade apart (the 1920s and the 1950s, for example). Make copies of five images of women from each decade, then lay them next to similar images from recently published magazines and books. Look at figure shapes (for example, voluptuous and heavy or pencil-thin), height, breast size, amount of makeup, and how the model is posed to make her seem more attractive (such as twisting her body). Also notice the fashions, as styles were meant to emphasize the beauty ideals of the time. What are your conclusions?

Protest a Pageant

By emphasizing the way women look in bathing suits and glamorous evening gowns, beauty pageants reinforce the idea that women are mainly valuable as beauty objects. There *is* such a thing as being too thin, and you see it in contestants. According to a 2003 Rutgers University study, 26 percent of pageant contestants in the last eighty years have been so thin that they qualified as undernourished by World Health Organization standards.

But thanks to protests by women and girls, some pageants (such as those in small towns) have been attracting fewer contestants and getting fewer sponsors. Former model Ann Simonton made a real impact when she created "Myth California" pageants, which occurred outside the actual pageants and used creative, funny tactics. Once, when Simonton wore a thirty-pound evening dress made entirely of bologna, she was mistaken as a contestant. Another year, she wore a bathing suit made of raw steak and a pageant-style "Miss Steak" banner to make the point that pageants treat women like pieces of meat.

If you want to help get rid of a pageant, start at your local level. Find out when a qualifying pageant will be held in your area by contacting the Miss America organization (609-345-7571) or Miss Universe (producers of Miss Universe, Miss USA, and Miss Teen USA; 212-373-4999, missupr@missuniverse.com). Then write a letter to the editor of your local newspaper expressing your thoughts about pageants. The point is to educate people who might not be aware of these contests' negative effect on women.

Next step: Protest! Citizens are allowed to picket and distribute information as long as they don't block entryways or exits and they aren't on private property. City streets and sidewalks are public property. This means you and your friends have every right to exercise free speech outside a pageant. Get a group together to make signs and hand out flyers. The more people involved, the bigger your impact.

Mad About Modeling

By AUDREY D. BRASHICH ★ New York, New York

When I was growing up, I dreamed the dream: I wanted to be a model because I thought it would be a surefire way of getting power and recognition for myself. I envisioned a life of glamorous parties and hot guys with myself as the star.

I first modeled when I was two, posing with Santa for an organization's Christmas card. At age five I appeared in *Modern Bride,* modeling flower-girl fashions at a fake wedding ceremony. Everyone on the set—the hair and makeup artists, the photographer, and his assistant—fawned over me, and in the published photos, it's obvious that people had been telling me how cute I was all day long.

Even when I wasn't the most beautiful girl in the room, people were impressed by the mere fact that I'd modeled. So when *Seventeen* held a call for models at my high school, I was convinced that if I could get chosen, it would make everyone want to date me or be my best friend forever. It didn't. In fact, when I was the only girl from my school selected to model for the magazine, I was shunned by most of my girlfriends. No one wanted to be around someone with the label that automatically got boys' attention: *model.*

When I got older and became an editor at *YM* and *Jump,* I opened thousands of letters from girls writing things like, "I beg you to please consider me next time your magazine is looking for new faces," and "I secretly I long to be an actress or model. I want to know I'm beautiful . . . someone is only beautiful when other people think they are." These teens were looking for the cultural affirmation that's showered on models—attention that most female artists, politicians, social workers, Nobel Prize winners, and mothers never receive. And no wonder: images in movies, TV shows, music videos, and magazines all suggest that being discovered as a model is the best thing that could ever happen to a girl.

All those desperate letters, combined with my own experiences as a model, made me think twice about what I was doing. I hated giving up a piece of my individuality every time a makeup artist made me over to fit her idea of what I should look like. I decided that instead of continuing to be a model, I wanted to help change the way people think about modeling. Because when it comes right down to it, it's so much cooler to be known for doing good than for looking good.

Audrey D. Brashich is the author of UnStarStruck (Walker Books, 2005), a book about how the cultural status of models, stars, and "celebutantes" affects young women. Her Web site is www.unstarstruck.com.

GOOD NEWS

In response to complaints that Mattel's unrealistic-looking Barbie doll (her measurements were 38-14-34) was bad for girls' self-images, Mattel did "plastic surgery" on selected versions of the doll. Barbie emerged with a thicker waist, smaller breasts, and less curviness.

Cool Quote

**When you['ve] got joy on the inside it shows on the out.
Be confident and you're beautiful without a doubt.**

—SALT-N-PEPA, rap group

The Gardener and the Tree

Once upon a time, there was a gardener who loved small trees. He didn't like trees that were tall and full—only small and dainty ones—and he planted all varieties of them in his grove. One year he noticed a young tree coming up that he hadn't planted. Normally, he grew only trees that he had carefully selected, but this tree's leaves were a nice almond shape and its trunk had a nice texture and lovely coloring, so he decided to let it stay.

The tree grew, and the gardener became unhappy because it wasn't small like the others but had a large trunk and full branches. So he decided that he would make this tree small like the others. First he chopped off its long and bushy branches and cut its trunk to a shorter height. Then he stopped giving it water as regularly as he did the other trees and built a shade around it so that it wouldn't get so much sun. He believed that if he held back nourishment, the tree would stop growing and become small and dainty like the other trees in his grove.

Gradually the tree did stop growing, but instead of becoming a small dainty tree, it became a large tree that never grew. Its trunk was full and ready to support many branches, but they had all been cut away. The sparse new growth it had managed to generate without proper sun and water was spindly and unhealthy.

One day when the gardener stopped by, he saw that the bark had lost its lovely coloring and the leaves had become thin and curled. The trunk that had been large and tall now looked silly at the shorter height. The gardener shook his head sadly and said, "What have I done? Instead of creating the tree I wanted, I have ruined the tree I had."

—from *Coping with a Negative Body Image*, by Kathy Bowen-Woodward

FOR MORE INFORMATION

Dying to Be Thin, www.pbs.org/wgbh/nova/thin. The Web site for *Dying to Be Thin*, a TV program originally broadcast in 2000. You can view the program right on the site.

Eating Disorder Referral and Information Center, www.EDReferral.com. Need help? This site gives you names and locations of counselors who specialize in eating disorders.

Fat! So?: Because You Don't Have to Apologize for Your Size, by Marilyn Wann (Ten Speed, 1999). A thought-provoking, funny read by an activist fighting "fear of fat."

The Looks Book: A Whole New Approach to Beauty, Body Image, and Style, by Rebecca Odes, Esther Drill, and Heather McDonald (Penguin, 2002). An in-depth look at appearance presented in a fun format.

Media Watch, www.mediawatch.com. Founder Ann Simonton has lots of ideas for protesting beauty pageants and increasing awareness of how images demean women.

National Association of Anorexia Nervosa and Associated Disorders, Box 7, Highland Park, IL 60035; 847-831-3438, www.anad.org. Provides free services including referrals to counselors and self-help groups.

National Eating Disorders Association, 603 Stewart St., Suite 803, Seattle, WA 98101; 206-382-3587, 800-931-2237 (help or referrals), www.nationaleatingdisorders.org. Check out their cool Web site.

No Body's Perfect: Stories by Teens about Body Image, Self-Acceptance, and the Search for Identity, by Kimberly Kirberger (Scholastic, 2002).

Real Gorgeous: The Truth about Body & Beauty, by Kaz Cooke (Norton, 1996). A funny book written to help girls and women gain a broader perspective on our beauty-obsessed culture.

Something Fishy Website on Eating Disorders, www.something-fishy.org. Support for conquering an eating disorder, danger signs, and lots of helpful info.

Chapter 3

You Go, Girl!

Imagine an adult telling a twelve-year-old girl to calm down, talk more softly, or stop goofing off. Now picture the same scene, but with a boy. Which is more likely?

Boys are allowed and even *expected* to be rambunctious. After all, people say, "Boys will be boys." By contrast, girls who show the same energy levels don't get, "Oh well, 'girls will be girls'"; instead they're reminded to be "ladylike." So while boys become comfortable being the center of attention, girls learn to quiet down and fade out.

Believe it or not, it used to be considered inappropriate for a woman even to *whistle*, as author Laurel King notes in her book *A Whistling Woman Is Up to No Good*. Women who whistled were clearly not inhibited or afraid to be noticed; since they were "untamed," they were considered a threat to society (some were even burned at the stake for it). As recently as the early twentieth century, female whistling was still considered brash. Now whistling is no big deal, and women have been encouraged to get in touch with their "wild" side, but some girls and women still don't feel okay making a commotion of *any* kind.

Get comfortable with this concept if you aren't already. If you're someone who naturally talks loudly, sounds off, sings, or makes your presence felt in any other ways, then don't silently shrink away. You have every right to stand out. And when you do this as an expression of your true self, your life is bound to be more rewarding. "Your playing small doesn't serve the world," explains author Marianne

Williamson. "There's nothing enlightened about shrinking so that other people won't feel insecure around you. We are all meant to shine, as children do. . . . And as we let our own light shine, we unconsciously give others permission to do the same."

THINGS TO DO

Reclaim Your Original Self (If You've Lost It)

Think about how you behaved in the past, both around individuals, such as friends and family members, and in groups. Have you always had lots to say? Have you been talkative only when something's fired you up? Or have you been most in your natural state when keeping to yourself? Compare how you behave now with the way you were in the past. See if you've been editing yourself. If so, stop it! You have nothing to lose by being your authentic self.

Cultivate a Sense of Adventure

Have you ever wanted to do something a little bold or different but you squelched the urge because of what people might think? Next time that urge strikes, indulge it. Pick an outdoor activity that sounds interesting and persuade a friend or parent to enjoy it with you. Go on a hike or a bike ride, enter a skateboarding contest, see if there's an Outward Bound ropes course in your area (ropes courses are especially great for building your self-confidence; see page 23). Being adventurous and making regular excursions out into the world is not only good for your health and well-being, it freshens up your life and makes it more fun.

Celebrate Fabulous Females

Some history books may give you the impression that through the ages, women have generally been soft-spoken, passive observers, patiently waiting behind while men go do the exciting things. Don't buy it. Generations of active, dynamic, outspoken, energetic women have made their marks on the world. Learn about some of these stars of the past. For starters, read about Dorothy Parker, Mother Jones, Susan B. Anthony, and Annie Oakley. And while you're at it, notice the cool accomplished women of today. Find out what Susan Sarandon, Jodie Foster, Carol Jenkins, Eileen Fisher, Katie Couric, and Salma Hayek have done lately. All of this "study" is sure to inspire you to stand out yourself.

Climbing Lessons

By ANDREA FLOYD, Fourteen ★ Sebastopol, California

A lot of people don't understand rock climbing. I used to be one of them. Like the average person, I cringed at the thought of hanging by my fingertips on a steep rock face with nothing between me and the ground except air. I felt that it was a boring thing guys do to try to prove they're macho. The guys I knew wore a strange-looking harness with a rope attached to it, jammed their hands and feet into a bunch of little pockets in a rock, and called it fun!

Once I tried climbing, however, everything changed. For one thing, I learned a valuable lesson: You shouldn't prejudge people or activities, because you can miss out on some pretty amazing experiences. I also learned that some women have become very well known as professional climbers, and I learned that girls can climb just as well as guys.

I set out to climb my first rock with my brother when I was thirteen. People thought I was kind of crazy, and I felt like I was doing something daring. I was intimidated by the prospect of ever getting up that wall, but I overcame the fear and kept at it. Toward the end of the summer, my dad, brother, and I went on a climbing trip to the eastern Sierras, which are beautiful mountains. It was here that I knew climbing was for me.

Climbing is both challenging and relaxing. When you're thirty feet up, you're forced to think about getting to the top, not about the stress of school and everyday life. It is physically and mentally rewarding. Most important, it has affected my life in positive ways—giving me a new sense of confidence and respect for myself. I'm glad I took a chance on it, and I know that it will continue to be one of my passions and a source of inspiration for me for many years to come.

We do something dumb,
completely ridiculous,
we laugh hysterically for
    20 minutes.
People who are not included
involved think we are crazy,
immature, obnoxious.
It's hard for them to understand
the fun we have when

we're with each other
because they're our own
    games, our own group.
We can also be serious.
They sometimes can't
    understand our problems.
Why are we so upset about
    coming in
    at 10 o'clock.

We are good support for each
    other.
Just having your friends near
makes everything easier.

 —CECELIA MANLEY,
teen, from *Almost Grown*

The Power of Laughter

By ROZ WARREN ★ Bala Cynwyd, Pennsylvania

If you're the kind of girl who likes to goof around, crack jokes, or make fun of things, you're doing something right. Humor is very powerful stuff. Everybody loves to laugh, and if you can make others laugh, that makes you valuable to them.

Sometimes people—particularly guys—find funny girls threatening. They're probably scared that if you have a sharp wit, you could end up turning it on *them*. Maybe that's why our culture gives girls the message that it's "unfeminine" to crack jokes and laugh. When a boy says a girl has a good sense of humor, sometimes what he really means is that she laughs at his jokes (whether they're funny or not), not that *her* jokes make him laugh.

But being able to laugh and make fun of things that deserve to be mocked is one of the best things you can do. Not only is it fun, being able to laugh makes you stronger. I'm not saying that you've got to run around grinning all the time. Sometimes it's difficult to find anything to laugh about. But if you can manage not to lose your sense of humor, it can help you get through rough times. Laughter is a real survival mechanism. Don't let anyone talk you out of it!

Roz Warren edits and publishes humor books for women, including Women's Lip: Outrageous, Irreverent and Just Plain Hilarious Quotes.

Cool Quotes

 One can never consent to creep when one feels an impulse to soar.

—HELEN KELLER, writer, lecturer

Women have been taught to speak softly and carry a lipstick. Those days are over.

—BELLA ABZUG, lawyer, politician, activist

FOR MORE INFORMATION

Girls Who Rocked the World and *Girls Who Rocked the World 2*, by Michelle Roehm McCann (Beyond Words, 2000). Stories of amazing feats that girls accomplished before the age of twenty.

Gutsy Girls: Young Women Who Dare, by Tina Schwager and Michelle Schuerger (Free Spirit, 1999). True stories of courageous personal challenges plus ideas for things you can do.

More Spice Than Sugar, by Lillian Morrison (Houghton Mifflin, 2001). Features poems that will inspire you to challenge gender roles.

Outward Bound USA, National Office, 100 Mystery Point Road, Garrison, NY 10524; (866) 467–7651. Hosts coed and female-only outdoor adventure programs that help participants become more aware of themselves and their environment. Ages fourteen and up.

Picture the Girl: Young Women Speak Their Minds, by Audrey Shehyn (Hyperion, 2000). Teens share their thoughts and emotions in this book created by a photojournalist.

"Women Who Dare" postcards, Pomegranate Publications, Inc., P.O. Box 808022, Petaluma CA 94975-8022; 707-782-9000 or 800-227-1428, www.pomegranatecommunications.com. Cool women's card collections.

Chapter 4

Good Housekeeping

What do cooking, washing dishes, folding laundry, cleaning, and childcare have in common?

Yep, they've all traditionally been done by women and girls. In the mid-1900s, most American women were housewives, keeping things tidy while their husbands went to work. But now, many women have jobs, too. Does this mean housework is now shared equally by males and females? No . . . even when women work full-time, most are *also* the primary housekeepers. Basically, women work another whole workday after their shift at the office, according to Arlie Hochschild, author of *The Second Shift*. This imbalance affects your generation as well: Research shows that girls hold more responsibility for housework than boys. And according to a study at Swarthmore College, when girls start high school, their housework loads double from two to four hours a week. Meanwhile, high school boys have plenty of time to devote to their own activities and having fun.

In a family with two working parents, the housework can and should be shared between the parents, as well as among the sons and daughters. One bright note: In 1965, American men were responsible for about 14 percent of the housework and childcare; now they're doing around 39 percent, according to Liana C. Sayer. In addition, men have become more "emotionally involved" at home (they've become more affectionate with their kids, empathetic to people's feelings, and attentive to problems).

What Happens in YOUR Home?

Your family environment is a good place to study male and female roles. For example, if your mom's the sole chef, you might believe that mothers are *supposed* to cook. (Of course, if your mom loves to cook, it's not an issue.) Likewise, if your father or brother does most of the yard work, you might think of it as "men's work" even though your mom could do it just as well. Maybe you've seen the males in your household "forget" to do chores, pretend they don't know how, or do such a bad job that they aren't asked again.

Regardless of what you've come to expect, you can suggest changes in your household and ask your parents to support equal treatment. This may require some effort, but think of the rewards. And if you can have an impact at home, who knows what you'll do next?

Things To Do ———————————

Divide the Housework Fairly

Maybe you've got an incredible brother who routinely makes dinner or your dad is a single parent who keeps the entire household humming. If you do, celebrate this good fortune. If you don't, take heart and know that it's not hopeless. Assess how the chores are being done. Does your brother leave the house every time your parents ask for help cleaning up? If the housework isn't distributed evenly, ask your parents to remedy the situation by creating a chores chart (see next page). Even if the chart only calls attention to the fact that some family members aren't pulling their weight, that's a start.

1. Make a list of all the chores.
2. Give each chore a point value from 1 to 4 based on the time and involvement it requires (1 is an easy task; 4 is a big deal).
3. Look at the sample chart below and draw up one for your family.
4. For the upcoming week, divide the chores so each person's points add up as equally as possible (it's okay if the totals vary a little).
5. List each person's duties in a separate column.
6. Put the chart in a central place, such as on the refrigerator.
7. Next week, rotate the sets of chores.

```
+---------------------------------------------------------------+
|        MOM              CHORES              DAD               |
|  Cooking, weeknights (4)              Mowing lawn (2)         |
|   Grocery shopping (1)   July 18-26   Cooking, weekends (3)   |
|                                                               |
|       SARAH             JEREMY              MARC             |
|  Dishes, weeknights (3)           Feeding dog every day (3)  |
|   Taking out trash (2)  Dishes, weekends (2)   Dusting (1)   |
|                          Laundry (3)       Vacuuming (1)     |
+---------------------------------------------------------------+
```

Note: If someone prefers a particular job (for example, if you love to mow the lawn) and no one minds, let that person do that chore on a regular basis.

Discover the Fun of Fixing Things

How much do you rely on yourself, and how much do you rely on other people? Boys are generally encouraged to be self-sufficient, but many girls learn to ask for help and rely on guys (this is known as "learned helplessness"). If you want to be independent and resourceful—not to mention expand your options for household chores—start taking care of jobs that require tools such as a hammer and a drill.

One way to strengthen your do-it-yourself skills is to do projects and chores that your father, brother, or some other guy usually does. This could mean repairing broken furniture, replacing light bulbs, troubleshooting computer problems, working on and washing the car, painting, landscaping, or mowing the lawn.

"Outdoor work is not just boys' work," says John Moline of Duluth, Minnesota, the father of three boys and one girl, twelve-year-old Jill. He and Jill recently stripped and painted the fence around their yard. Not all the projects with her dad have been easy, but Jill thinks having a good attitude has helped. "Something might seem hard at first, but not after you start doing it," she says. And I like having time with my father."

"Trade Places" with Your Brother

Does your brother make light of women's rights ("Isn't everyone equal *already?*")? Maybe you can open his eyes a little. For one day (preferably on a weekend), ask him to "trade identities" with you so he can see what life's like for a girl (and you can see what it's like for a guy). Ask him to do basically what you do all day. Alert your parents so they can treat each of you as each other. Of course you'll have to be yourselves for certain activities, but try to get into the act.

At the end of the day, compare your experiences. Your brother may have gained some appreciation for what it means to be female, and you'll have gained new insight on male behavior. If your brother claims to have learned nothing, that's okay; interacting with him will make you stronger and more self-assured. And you may end up helping him after all. "I'm glad I have sisters who support women's rights," says Ryan Stanley, a college student in San Diego, California. "They helped me understand what girls and women have to deal with, and that's helped me in my relationships with women."

Tribute to My Brother

By BRAZLEY DARAJA, thirteen ★ Hempstead, New York

At my house we have a system for doing housework. Mom tries to keep it equally divided, and I think it's pretty fair. For dishes, I do them one week, my brother does them the next week, and my mom the third week. When someone is doing the dishes, the other is taking out the garbage. If I clean the living room, my brother cleans the bathroom.

I'm glad we have it organized this way. At some of my friends' houses, the girls do the dishes and their brothers don't. The boys do the "boy stuff," like taking out the garbage and washing the car. That's not fair, because cleaning the house is hard. Taking out a bag of garbage a day is nothing compared to doing the dishes from breakfast, lunch, and dinner. Washing the car every now and then is easy!

It wasn't always this way at my house. My brother used to say he didn't have to do the dishes because he's a boy. My mom would tell him that men aren't better than women, and then he would have to do them for another week! I don't know where he got it, but he had this idea that women belong in the kitchen. He said when he grows up, he's going to wear the pants in the family and his wife is going to stay home with the children. I told him I thought he'd been watching too much Al Bundy. So we started fighting. He pushed me, but I just beat him up because I'm stronger.

Now that he's ten and I'm thirteen, we don't argue as much anymore (his punches hurt now!) and we're able to talk about problems. My mom and I got those chauvinistic ideas out of his head. Now he'll even volunteer to do the dishes. If it's my turn to do them and I want to go to the mall, he'll say he'll do them for me. Once I asked him, "Do I have to pay you back?" And he said no.

He really believes that it's a good thing to share the housework and to be equal in other ways. For example, once he and I were at my friend's house. In response to a question from my friend, her mom said, "You know you have to ask your father about that because he's the boss." My brother asked, "How come? Why aren't you in charge? What makes him better?" My friend's mom just looked at me. I was surprised and embarrassed. But afterward I told my brother I was glad he said it. We need more boys like him in the world!

Make a Female Family Tree

People typically trace their ancestry through the male lineage, which gives the female half short shrift. Tracing your family's female roots can be fascinating, giving you new perspective on who you are. Find out who the women in your family were—what was important to them, and what challenges did they face? Ask your parents what they know, and take notes. Did anyone save journals or letters they may have written? Once you've dug up everything you can find, make a family-tree diagram. Include any photos of your great-grandmother, grandmother, mother, sisters, and yourself. Then write a couple of paragraphs on each woman. "Once you discover the voices and actions of the women in your family, you're reminded that you're connected to a lineage," says Jan Stoltman, a writer and coach. "It's very liberating. . . . You can carry that power forward."

Housework

You know, there are times
    when we happen to be
just sitting there quietly
    watching TV,
when the program we're
    watching will stop for a while
and suddenly someone
    appears with a smile
and starts to show us
    how terribly urgent
it is to buy some brand
    of detergent
        or soap
        or cleanser
        or cleaner
        or powder
        or paste
        or wax
        or bleach—
to help with the housework.
Now, most of the time
    it's a lady we see
who's doing the housework
    on TV.

She's cheerfully scouring
    a skillet or two,
or she's polishing pots
    'til they gleam like new,
or she's scrubbing the tub,
    or she's mopping the floors,
or she's wiping the stains
    from the walls and the doors,
or she's washing the windows,
    the dishes, the clothes,
or cleaning the "fridge,"
    or the stove or the sink
with a lighthearted smile
    and a friendly wink
and she's doing her best
    to make us think
that *her* soap
        (or detergent
        or cleanser
        or cleaner
        or powder
        or paste
        or wax
        or bleach)

is the best one
that there is in the whole wide world!

And maybe it is . . .
and maybe it isn't . . .
and maybe it does what they
    say it will do . . .
but I'll tell you one thing
    I *know* is true:

The lady we see
    when we're watching TV—
the lady who smiles
    as she scours
        or scrubs
        or rubs
        or washes
        or wipes
        or mops
        or dusts
        or cleans—
or whatever she does
on our TV screens—
that lady is smiling because she's an actress.
And she's earning money
for learning those speeches
that mention those wonderful
        soaps
        and detergents
        and cleansers
        and cleaners
        and powders
        and pastes
        and waxes
        and bleaches.
So the very next time
    you happen to be
just sitting there quietly
    watching TV,

and you see some nice lady
    who smiles as
she scours
        or scrubs
        or rubs
        or washes
        or wipes
        or mops
        or dusts
        or cleans
    remember:
Nobody smiles doing housework
but those ladies you see on TV.
Because even if
the soap
        or detergent
        or cleanser
        or cleaner
        or powder
        or paste
        or wax
        or bleach
that you use
    is the very best one—
housework
    is just no fun.

Children,
when you have a house of your own
make sure, when there's housework to do,
that you don't have to do it alone.
Little boys, little girls,
when you're big husbands and wives,
if you want all the days of your lives
to seem sunny as summer weather
make sure, when there's housework to do,
that you do it together.

—SHELDON HARNICK,
in *Free to Be You and Me*

The Story of Cinderella...

GOOD NEWS

Does all that housework really even NEED doing? According to WORKING MOTHER magazine, 25 percent of Americans no longer scrub floors, 20 percent don't wash windows, and 33 percent have quit ironing.

Cool Quote

When I was ten, I was told somebody's got to clean the fish. Well, my idea of feminism is that everyone cleans the fish.

—CYNDI LAUPER, singer

FOR MORE INFORMATION

Free to Be You and Me, by Marlo Thomas and Friends (Running Press, 2002). Stories, songs, and poems about being yourself and being a member of a family.

Chapter 5

Take That!

Most of the guys in your life are probably kind, caring, respectful, and nonviolent toward you. Unfortunately, some men and boys aren't. They abuse women and girls verbally, emotionally, physically, and/or sexually. According to the *Journal of the American Medical Association*, 20 percent of adolescent girls are subjected to physical or sexual abuse from their intimate partner.

Part of the problem is that our society—in the form of entertainment and advertising—conveys the idea that it's okay to demean and control women. Female abuse—or even just the idea of it—is made to seem commonplace. And this can affect people's attitudes, for example, by degrading boys' respect for the girls and women in their lives.

Activist groups such as the National Organization for Women (NOW) have had some success in their quest to end gender-related violence. A 1998 law called the Violence Against Women Act (VAWA) provided funding for programs that deal with sexual assault. More still needs to be done, but the most important thing you can do right now is to look out for your own safety. It pays to know how to stay out of a potentially violent or abusive situation, and how to defend yourself if you're in one. You need to be prepared, both mentally and physically, just in case.

THINGS TO DO

Be Date Safe

Before you go on a date with a guy, your own safety is probably not your main concern. You're no doubt thinking about what you're going to wear, what you'll talk about, and whether he'll like you. These are natural things to ponder, but keep safety in mind, too. You can have a good time and still look out for yourself:

★ **When you first go out with someone, double-date.** Your date may turn out to be completely trustworthy, but you can discover that as you get to know each other.

★ **Observe your date's behavior, both in general and toward you.** How does he talk about girls or women? How does he treat you? If he doesn't listen well, seems angry at women, or talks about girls in a degrading way, he might have psychological issues that would make him a bad boyfriend.

★ **Pay close attention to any warnings from your intuition.** Many girls and young women who've been assaulted have reported afterward that a little voice inside told them not to agree to go on a date or get in the car with the person. Don't ignore input from your sixth sense. If you're not sure about someone, it's always better to err on the side of safety.

★ **Don't put up with any guy who doesn't treat you right.** No matter how cute he is or how much you want to be with him, your safety and well-being should always come first. If you're being verbally, emotionally, or physically threatened or abused, don't wait another day—run away.

Take a Self-Defense Class

The single most constructive thing you can do to protect yourself is to learn self-defense. According to the U.S. Department of Justice and research by Sarah Ullman, while it's sometimes best not to fight, such as when the assailant has a gun, in general, physically resisting an attack increases your odds of surviving.

A self-defense class will show you how to decrease your chances of being assaulted in the first place, and how to fight off attack through basic physical techniques. You'll discover where your greatest strengths lie (for example, girls and women have incredible power in their legs and hips). Perhaps most important, this class will boost your self-confidence, surprise you with how strong you are, and give you a take-charge attitude that says "Don't mess with me."

"Girls and women are socialized to put others first, which is a setup for victimization," says Helen Grieco, a self-defense teacher and National Organization for Women (NOW) activist. "We're taught we aren't capable of hurting another human being, but that's a myth. Taking self-defense and learning that you're worth defending can positively transform your life."

Many local communities offer "street safety" self-defense courses, and some have classes especially for teen girls. You can also develop self-defense related skills by taking a martial arts class such as karate or tae kwon do. How do you find a class? Call the local women's center, look in the yellow pages under *Martial Arts*, or contact Model Mugging, www.modelmugging.com, 1222 Magnolia Avenue #105-202, Corona, CA 92881-2075, 800-590-4687.

Train Your Brain

It's empowering to know that you can defend yourself physically. But it's also key to be prepared *mentally*—to think about how you'd react *before* you're in a situation where you might have to fight back. Helen Benedict, author of *Safe, Strong & Streetwise*, suggests these "mental self-defense" tips:

★ **Trust your instincts.** This can't be overstated!

★ **Believe in your power and strength.** You're probably much stronger and faster than you realize (as you'll discover when you take self-defense).

★ **Picture how you'd respond if someone tried to assault you.** What are your best defensive assets? If you have a loud voice, yelling might be ideal. If you have strong legs, kicking the attacker or stomping on his feet might be most effective.

★ **Determine what's scaring you.** If you're in or approaching a situation that makes the hair on the back of your neck stand on end, figure out why (if it's not obvious). What can you do to feel more secure? For example, if you're having doubts about walking through a dark area at night, can a friend walk with you?

★ **If you are attacked, keep calm.** Try to take deep breaths and stay alert for ways to escape.

Speak Out on Sexual Assault

People rarely talk about sexual violence, and this silence fosters a social atmosphere that avoids the problem and shuns victims. Help change this by discussing sexual assault with people to increase awareness; protesting jokes, entertainment, and ads that glorify violence and make women look sexually victimized; and helping victims stop or escape the abuse and seek counseling. If you feel strongly about this issue and want to take more of a leadership role, invite a personal-safety expert to discuss sexual assault at your school, church, or community group. To line up a speaker, call the local police department and ask if an officer is assigned to talk to groups on this topic. If no one is available, ask to be referred to a sexual-assault crisis center.

How I Fought Back

By DANIAL DUNLAP, seventeen ★ San Francisco, California

I got interested in taking self-defense when this guy had a "fatal attraction" to me. I was being stalked—he was following me to work and home, and I was afraid. Then he got a young woman to follow me, maybe because he knew I wouldn't be as cautious with her. She approached me one night when I was walking home, and when I was a block from my house, she said "This is from [his name]," and hit me in the face with a wrench.

I heard about a self-defense class from a woman who taught classes nearby, and I signed up. The teacher taught it with a male partner who dressed up in protective padding so we could practice hitting and kicking him. I learned to be more aware of my surroundings when I'm out in public and to recognize the signs that someone is dangerous or could want to hurt me. I learned how to do heel palms, back kicks, knee kicks, eye gouging, scratching, elbow throws, and ground fighting. I learned how to shake free when somebody grabs you from behind, to scream in their ear, and to get someone off of me if I'm pinned down. We also practiced the scenario of responding to an attacker who has a knife.

I also learned that just because guys are strong, they won't necessarily have the upper hand. Guys may be heavier and stronger than girls, but I learned that girls can do certain techniques to knock them out and get them down so they can get away. I hadn't realized some basic things could be defensive moves, like stepping on someone's foot. I knew it would hurt, but if you step on it a certain way, you can disable the attacker.

You know how you see a crazy person on the street, and you move faster and cross the street to get away? When I see someone like that now, I walk past without being afraid. I feel I can successfully defend myself against anybody who threatens me. This has changed my whole attitude about myself and given me a new sense of power and confidence. I recommend that every girl take self-defense!

I fight like a girl who knows that
THIS BODY and THIS MIND are mine.
I fight like a girl who knows that
YOU ONLY HAVE AS MUCH POWER
AS I GRANT YOU.
I fight like a girl who will
never allow you to take more than I offer.
I fight like a girl who fights back.

So next time you think you can distract
yourself
from your insecurities by victimizing a girl,
THINK AGAIN.
She may be ME and
I FIGHT LIKE A GIRL.
—ANONYMOUS,
from "I Fight Like a Girl"

GOOD NEWS

In 2002, California became the first state to allow victims of domestic violence and sexual assault to file civil charges against their attackers. Congress had approved this type of legislation in 1994, but the U.S. Supreme Court ruled that it was up to each state to decide. Will other states follow? California is a bellwether (trendsetter) state, so activists are hopeful.

FOR MORE INFORMATION

Domestic Violence Information Pages, King County, Washington, www.metrokc.gov/dvinfo. An excellent place to turn for quick facts.

Everything You Need to Know About Abusive Relationships, by Nancy N. Rue (Rosen Publishing Group, 1998).

He's Not All That! How to Attract the Good Guys, by Dr. Gilda Carle (Cliff Street Books, 2000). Loads of common sense and inspiration.

In Love and in Danger: A Teen's Guide to Breaking Free of Abusive Relationships by Barrie Levy (Seal Press, 1998). A workbook-style guide with personal stories and effective strategies.

Love Doesn't Have to Hurt Teens, www.apa.org/pi/pii/teen/homepage.html. The American Psychological Association runs this easy-to-read site with tips for safe dating.

Michigan Coalition Against Domestic and Sexual Violence, Health Promotion Clearinghouse, 111 W. Edgewood Blvd., Suite 11, Lansing, MI 48911, 800-353-8227. www.mcadsv.org/mrcdsv/resource/Bibliographies/Brochures.pdf. Free brochures on dating and domestic violence.

At School

❋ ❋ ❋ ❋ ❋ ❋ ❋ ❋ ❋ ❋ ❋ ❋ ❋ ❋

Chapter 6

Class Acts

School is where you go to classes, learn, take tests, and see friends. And, in some cases, it's where you deal with sexism. If your school is a shining example of equality, you're in luck. If not, this chapter is for you.

Textbooks

Although there's been a major campaign (and some people feel that it's gone too far) to free textbooks of all types of bias, many books still feature more male characters in the text and show more boys and men in the pictures. Textbooks may also present unbalanced views of history and current events. According to a report by the American Association of University Women (AAUW), women still represent only two to three percent of the people described in newer history textbooks. In some cases, men *have* been more prominent in history than women, but women's experiences and contributions to history have still been largely ignored. "When textbooks refer to women being 'given the vote' in 1920 but omit the challenges in that seventy-two-year struggle . . . they are imbalanced," explains Susan Crawford in *Beyond Dolls & Guns: 101 Ways to Help Children Avoid Gender Bias.*

Teachers

As you know if yours have been stellar, your teachers can be sources of inspiration and guidance. Good teachers strive to treat students equally, encourage you to share your thoughts in class discussions, and generally try to make you feel smart and confident about your future. If you have teachers you'd rate A+, let them know you appreciate their efforts.

Unfortunately, there are also teachers who do the opposite. They may ignore you during class discussions and subtly put down girls and women, making you feel just average. This might be because they've received little or no training in how to treat girls equally. Or they could be operating on an outdated belief, such as: "Boys need to do well in school so they can get good jobs and support their families, but girls don't need that because they'll be raising children."

A few teachers are blatantly sexist. For example, when she was in junior high school, author Peggy Orenstein (who wrote *Schoolgirls*) used a math book written by two men and a woman named Mary P. Dolciani. "Whenever there was a typo or a problem that didn't work out right, my teacher would say, 'Mary P. must've written that problem,'" says Orenstein. New York writer Miranda Van Gelder had a teacher who called all the girls Beautiful, Adorable, or Gorgeous. "I finally confronted him after class one day," she wrote in *Ms.* magazine, asking "if it was really too much to drop all the honey-cookie-pieface-lambchop stuff."

Then there's innocent gender bias that teachers aren't intending, such as choosing all boys for the cool projects. Most teachers don't want *anything* to do with sexism, will go out of their way to be fair, and would be embarrassed if they were discovered to favor boys in any way. But studies show that some well-meaning teachers pay less attention to girls and praise them less than boys in class. Why? Girls tend to be quiet and well behaved, thinking through their answers before raising their hands. Boys tend to be louder and rowdier, calling out answers much more often. In this atmosphere, it's not surprising that teachers focus on these "higher-maintenance" students or call on the first person with a hand up, who's usually a boy. Teachers have also been found to accept boys' answers when they call out but reprimand girls when *they* call out.

THINGS TO DO ————————————

Grade Your Books

How are the lessons in your textbooks presented? Make copies of the checklist on page 43, then fill out one for each book.

What can you do if your books are lacking in female representation? Start with your school. Ask teachers to either supplement the biased books with materials such as magazine articles or get new books. Point out images that need to be brought into the twenty-first century. Sometimes a simple suggestion will lead to changes.

Want to go a step further? Textbooks go through an elaborate screening process on the way to your school and your desk. First the state approves books from which school districts can select titles. School districts form committees that include school staff and members of the community, and these groups choose the books. Here's where you come in. If you have a beef with a book, write a letter to your school board and send a copy to the state curriculum commission (the address is in the government pages of the telephone book). Ask your friends, parents, and teachers to also write letters. There's a good possibility that the committee will choose to replace the book.

How Do Your Textbooks Rate?

Use this checklist to evaluate your textbooks. Make a copy of this page for each book or write your answers on a separate sheet of paper.

1. How many pictures in the book show only boys or men?_____

2. How many pictures show only girls or women?_____

3. What are the boys or men in the pictures doing? (List five activities.)

4. What are the girls or women in the pictures doing? (List five activities.)

5. How many major female figures or characters are in the book? _____

6. How many major male figures or characters?_____

ABOUT YOUR RESULTS

Questions 1–3: It's only fair that there should be just as many pictures of girls and women as boys and men.
Questions 4–5: If the girls and women are always doing passive things such as helping males or watching them work, the book is biased. Girls should be shown in active roles because they're just as capable of solving problems and taking action. And boys should be shown doing things such as helping a girl with a project or watching something happen—boys aren't always in charge.
Questions 6–7: Ideally, textbooks should include an equal number of males and females. The exception is history books; if men truly were the only ones involved, because, for instance, women weren't allowed to participate, that shouldn't be distorted.

Write to Your Book's Publisher

Another plan of action is to write to the company that publishes your textbook (look for the address on the copyright page or in the directory *Books in Print* at your local library). Here's a sample letter showing what you could say.

June 30, 2005

Nora Thompson
1415 Georgina Ave.
Monterey, CA 93940

ABC Publishing
123 Book Square
Minneapolis, MN 64572

Dear Publisher,

I think THE HISTORY OF MAN (2005), by John Smith and Steve Jones, is biased against girls and women in several ways.

First, shouldn't it be called THE HISTORY OF HUMANITY? The word "man" excludes half the population. Also, I did an informal survey of the number of male and female figures in the pictures and text, and there are a lot more males. Plus, when you show girls and women, they're doing things such as stirring the kettle (page 53) or striking a pose while men solve problems (page 79). The text says things like "The men who made America what it is today . . ." as though women were totally uninvolved bystanders, when in fact they made major contributions, even if what they did wasn't widely recognized.

Textbooks help shape kids' impressions of how life is and how it should be, so THE HISTORY OF MAN should have strong female role models. In the next edition please include more females as leaders and in active, influential roles. And why not also show some boys and men in less stereotypical roles—for example, preparing meals, taking care of children, and assisting women and girls? The book could also include more details about women's achievements in history.

Thank you for your consideration. I look forward to the next edition of the book.

Sincerely,
Nora Thompson, age eleven

Help a Teacher Be Fair

Do you have a teacher who treats you or other girls differently from the boys? Identify the specific offending behavior, such as saying degrading things about women, ignoring you when you raise your hand, or letting boys lead all the fun activities. Try to determine whether she's knowingly being unreasonable or is

Thanks, Ms. Logan

By JOSH HANER, fourteen ★ San Francisco, California

When I began middle school, I had a teacher named Judy Logan. One of her personal goals was to emphasize women in the curriculum. Her classroom had an amazing assortment of things in it—quilts, posters, and books all on women in our history. Some teachers ignore women's role in our culture, but not Ms. Logan. Instead she stressed female leaders and how they've actually been more important than they seem in our sheltered outlook on history.

For example, when I was in sixth grade, she had us give first-person oral histories of African-American historical figures—one male and one female. We also studied women in science and made a quilt depicting these scientific masters of their time. For one classroom assignment, Ms. Logan had us imagine that we were going back to our birth and were then born as the opposite sex. Later on, when I was in seventh grade, she offered a class on women in history. I decided to sign up, but I silently wondered if I would be the only boy.

The class actually had about the same number of girls and boys and turned out to be something I would remember for a long time. First we listed things that we thought made our gender different from the other, and we then formed two circles. The boys, in the inner circle, read their answers first, while the girls, in the outer circle, listened as a respectful audience. Most of the boys "passed" on reading because we were all too shy to show our true emotions. Then the girls read about what was on their minds. Through this, the boys gained the ability to identify with the opposite sex, knowing what girls go through each day and how their lives are similar to and different from ours. The subject of sexual harassment in schools also came up, and we broke into committees that did investigative studies on it. When the class was over, none of us wanted it to end.

Of all the teachers I've had over the years, Ms. Logan was the one who really made a difference and changed my outlook on life. I also became aware of the struggles that women have gone through to gain their place in society today. Ms. Logan taught me to become sensitive to other people's views. Whether the difference between us is race, religion, or gender, we still deserve the same rights to be heard. So for all of these reasons and more, I would like to say thank you, Ms. Logan.

simply blind to the behavior. If it's unintended, your tactfully speaking up might open her eyes and make her glad to have the opportunity to repair the situation. When you approach her, try to include a compliment along with the feedback to balance it out. Think of how you'd feel as the recipient of your comments.

If you think the teacher's behavior *is* intentional, start by talking to one of your parents or another adult you trust to get their thoughts. Depending on what they say, you might either go ahead and approach the teacher or instead start keeping a written record of exactly what happens and on what dates, and then tell the principal about the behavior after school's out (so there's no question that you got the grade you deserved).

Your school should definitely know if a teacher isn't treating girls fairly. Your complaint may not be the first about the person, and a reprimand may be in order (some sexist teachers have even been fired).

Start a Girls' Rights Group at School

A Washington, D.C.-based organization called Gender PAC (which stands for Public Advocacy Coalition) runs a program called GenderYOUTH, which helps high schools tackle sexism. Its representatives—many of whom are former students—visit schools to oversee discussions about sexism (in forms such as bullying and harassment) and set up on-site advocacy groups. Ask your principal to visit their Web site (*www.gpac.org*) and invite them to your school.

Add Novels with Girl Heroines to Your "Required Reading"

You may rely on textbooks in classes, but they shouldn't be the only books you read. There are tons of fun novels that feature girls leading people to victory and saving the world! Check the library for the books listed at the end of this chapter and browse bookstores for brand-new titles.

GOOD NEWS

 A report called "How Schools Short-Change Girls" published in the early 1990s by the American Association of University Women focused attention on sexism in schools. One result: A 1994 law called the Gender Equity in Education Act gave schools and organizations millions of dollars to stamp out sexism through the replacement of textbooks, teacher training, and other strategies.

Cool Quote

 The acceptance of women as authority figures or as role models is an important step in female education. . . . It is this process of identification, respect, and then self-respect that promotes growth.

—JUDY CHICAGO, artist

FOR MORE INFORMATION

RECOMMENDED NOVELS

The Alice series, by Phyllis Reynolds Naylor (Bantam Doubleday Dell)

Anne of Green Gables, by L. M. Montgomery (Dell, 1998)

Finding My Voice, by Marie G. Lee (HarperTrophy, 2001)

The Girl with the White Flag, by Tomiko Higa (Kodansha International, 2003)

The Girl Who Owned a City, by O.T. Nelson (Laureleaf, 1977 — reissue)

Hope Was Here, by Joan Bauer (Puffin, 2002)

How My Private, Personal Journal Became a Bestseller, by Julia DeVillers (Dutton, 2004)

Letters from a Slave Girl, by Mary Lyons (Aladdin, 1996)

Little Women, by Louisa May Alcott (Grammercy, 1998)

Number the Stars, by Lois Lowry (Laureleaf, 1998)

The Princess Diaries, by Meg Cabot (HarperCollins Juvenile Books, 2001)

Red Scarf Girl, by Ji-li Siang (HarperTrophy, 1998)

Sarah Bishop, by Scott O'Dell (Scholastic, 1991)

Shabanu, Daughter of the Winds, by Suzanne Fisher Staples (Random House, 1991)

The Sisterhood of the Traveling Pants and *The Second Summer of the Sisterhood*, by Ann Brashares (Delacorte Press, 2003)

Speak, by Laurie Halse Anderson (Puffin, 2001)

The True Confessions of Charlotte Doyle, by Avi (Camelot, 1997)

Zeely, by Virginia Hamilton (Scott Foresman, 1993)

BIOGRAPHIES

Herstory: Women Who Changed the World, by Ruth Ashby and Deborah Gore Ohrn (Viking, 1995)

Remember the Ladies: 100 Great American Women, by Cheryl Harness (HarperTrophy, 2003)

Chapter 7

Math Myths and Science Fiction

Do you like math? How about science?

If you said yes to either or both of these questions, that's excellent. Read on to find out why.

If you said no, you're not alone. Maybe you just haven't felt drawn to figuring out equations, or you've heard kids talking about tough assignments and thought, "No way am I doing that!" But hang on a minute. Even if you can't imagine yourself as a science or math star, or you're afraid you might not be good at these subjects, you (yes, *you*) could surprise yourself. "When it comes to science, girls are every bit as capable as boys," says junior-high physical science teacher Doug Kirkpatrick of Walnut Creek, California. "A little encouragement and attention go a long way."

Once you get your feet wet in some classes, you could flat-out *love* math or science, or both. And then you won't be alone, either, because according to *60 Minutes*, junior high and high school girls are doing exceedingly well in these two subjects; considerably *better* than boys. More young women are going to college than young men, and many are continuing on to business or medical school. The trend is so pronounced that school principals and teachers are calling for special attention to help *boys* catch up. This is significant, considering that not too long ago, girls were actively steered away from math and science, as if they couldn't handle them.

Why, then, does this book have a chapter encouraging you to pursue math and science? Because women still make up only a measly 9 percent of America's engineers and 16 percent of its scientists, and relatively few women are earning degrees in engineering. What's more, the U.S. Bureau of Labor Statistics says there are increasingly more jobs in engineering, the natural sciences, and math. Translation: There's lots of room for you in these fields if you're interested.

So whether you're excited about math and science or a little reluctant, think seriously about them. Fall in love with algebra and geometry. Earn straight A's in calculus and chemistry. Discover the extent to which you can excel. Go out and become an engineer, scientist, doctor, or whatever other type of brainy professional you want.

On the Money

Great career opportunities are just one reason to pursue math and science. Another is the fact that jobs requiring some math or science aren't just interesting, they generally pay much better (and have more prestige) than traditionally female jobs that don't require much education, such as retail salesperson or salon worker. For instance, computer programming, a career that requires some math, generally pays more than sixty thousand dollars a year, while the average salary for secretarial work is about twenty-five thousand dollars.

THINGS TO DO ————————————

Take Those Classes!

No matter what you eventually decide to do with your life, make yourself eligible for the widest range of jobs: Enroll and do well in as many math and science classes as possible. If you want to go to college, you'll need at least one year of algebra and one of geometry. If you're interested in a science or engineering career, take trigonometry and calculus. One final suggestion: Take these subjects *as early as possible* to give yourself a head start. The sooner you get immersed in the material, the sooner you'll feel comfortable with it.

Ask Your Teachers for Help

If you're an A or B student in math and science, skip this section. If you aren't, you can increase your chances of succeeding by letting your teachers know you're interested in doing well, and by asking for help when you need it. Teachers love it when students express a genuine interest in what they're learning. If they know you care, they'll generally make an extra effort to help you understand the work. (If you feel shy, ask a classmate to tag along to make it more of a group discussion.)

Don't be afraid to ask for assistance. Science and math can be challenging for *anyone*—boys or girls. Even the smartest students struggle with certain subjects and assignments. Asking for help is not a sign of weakness; it's the most constructive thing you can do, and in some cases it's the only way to clear up confusion.

Organize a Girls' Math or Science Group

Do you find that it's easier to concentrate on math or science when boys aren't around? Some girls do better working one-on-one in a relaxed, all-female environment, since guys often dominate discussions and take up teachers' time. As a result, schools are starting to form all-girl study groups (and in some cases, entirely all-girl classes).

If you're in a coed math or science class and feel distracted or ignored, ask some of the other girls if they'd be interested in forming a study/activity group. Meet during lunch or after school one day a week and go over class material. Find a parent or teacher willing to work with you on extracurricular math- and science-related activities. One girls' science group in Newton, Massachusetts, has gone camping, stayed overnight at Boston's Museum of Science, visited a veterinary hospital, gone on nature hikes, collected algae from a pond and studied it under a microscope, and talked to female geology majors at nearby Wellesley College. "I never used to know *why* we were doing science experiments at school," says fifteen-year-old group member Liz Castellana. "What we do in the group shows me that there are reasons for doing the experiments—we think of logical questions and then answer them."

Get SMART

Give yourself a boost by signing up for a program called Operation SMART (Science, Math, and Relevant Technology), which is run by Girls Incorporated. At an Operation SMART center you do hands-on projects such as taking apart a computer, doing a chemistry experiment, or building a model city. These activities help girls "see that mistakes aren't failures but opportunities," says Girls Inc. "As they become confident inquirers and explorers, their enthusiasm for science, math, and all learning begins to grow. . . . They learn that they can have power over their lives and change the world around them." Contact Girls Inc. (see page 130) to see if there's an Operation SMART center near you.

Learn About Female Math and Science Whizzes

Do you have an assignment to study a historical figure? Instead of picking someone like George Washington or Albert Einstein, choose a scientist or mathematician such as Grace Hopper or Marie Curie. Not only will you expand your knowledge, you'll enlighten your classmates. You may not be able to think of many women mathematicians or scientists off the top of your head, but you'll find many in the biographies at the end of this chapter.

Explore Computers

That computer on your desk could lead you to a career as a software programmer, computer engineer, Web site designer, or Web writer. Start now discovering what you can do with that keyboard and screen. If your family owns a computer, you've probably already been sending and receiving e-mail, instant messaging, and talking in chat rooms*, and you know how to use software (such as word-processing and photo-editing programs). If you don't have a computer at home, check the local library.

Check Out Girl-Friendly Video Games

According to Laura Groppe, the CEO of an organization called Girls Intelligence Agency, girls make up forty percent of online game players. However, the video game industry doesn't seem to realize that the majority of video games labeled for girls are focused on appearance or playing with dolls (Barbie), and they don't help girls develop coordination or computer skills. In addition, many games that feature girl main characters have clearly been created for guys (such as *Dead or Alive Xtreme Beach Volleyball*), and these characters have unrealistically curvy and buxom bodies. "Sure, Lara Croft is a great archaeologist," says an editor at *YM* magazine, "but does she have to dress in that midriff-baring outfit with a chest that screams 'implants'?"

If you're like most girls, you want nonviolent games with some strategy and a plot beyond just conquering the evil enemy. If you'd like to see games that appeal to what you want, write to the companies and ask them to design better products for girls. Mention the titles you like and why they've entertained or helped you. Every letter a company receives will push its executives to think about how they can successfully sell to the girls' market.

* *Caution: Avoid strangers who approach you online just as you'd avoid them in real life.*

Meanwhile, you can still enjoy video games—not *everything* out there is terrible for girls and women. For example, *Downhill Domination* features female pro mountain bike riders. Here are others to try:

Dance Dance Revolution (Konami)

Daria's Inferno (and others in this series; Pearson Software)

Ecco the Dolphin (Acclaim)

Harry Potter and the Chamber of Secrets (and others in this series; Warner Home Video)

Mia Hamm Soccer and *Mia Hamm Soccer Shootout* (South Peak Interactive)

Nancy Drew: Stay Tuned for Danger (and others in this series; HerInteractive)

The Saddle Club (Atari)

WTA Tour Tennis (Konami)

Zoombinis Logical Journey (and others in this series; Learning Company)

Surf the Web

The Internet has become the primary database of our society (see www.google.com to confirm this), and there's a lot you can learn about math and science (or anything else) online. "I read *National Geographic* articles online," says Margaret Coit, twelve, of Lexington, Massachusetts. "I put up a question about a science project on one of the electronic bulletin boards, 'Homework Helper,' and got nineteen answers."

And while you're out there on the Web, make sure to check out the many wonderful Web sites created especially for you. Here are a few where you can get support on personal issues you're dealing with, learn about successful women, read girls' true-life stories, find pen pals, collect quotes, and follow links to more cool info.

Club Girl Tech, www.girltech.com

Feminist.com, www.feminist.com

Girls Incorporated, www.girlsinc.org

Girl Power!, www.girlpower.gov

GirlSite, www.girlsite.org

Girlstart, www.girlstart.com

A Girl's World, www.agirlsworld.com

Girl Zone, www.girlzone.com

New Moon, www.newmoon.org

SmartGirl, www.smartgirl.org

Math Notes

By ROBIN BERAN, fourteen ★ Aurora, Colorado

I go to Prairie Middle School in Aurora. My math teacher, Ms. Carpentar, formed a math club, and we compete against other math clubs in the Denver area. Ms. Carpentar is enthusiastic, energetic, and loves math. Miss Johnson, our student teacher, has also helped and encouraged us. At the beginning of the school year, we met once a week to play math games and solve riddles. Later in the year we competed against other schools.

Then came the metro competition. The judges were all people who use math and science in various industries every day. Some of the women had interesting jobs that I had never heard of. One woman worked with computers and made new computer games. They gave us the toughest test I have ever seen, and I've never worked harder… but Prairie was chosen to go to state competition. What's more, one team got an award for being all girls, and another girl won first place. I'm not the only girl who likes math!

FEMALE FIRST

NAME: Natalia Toro

In 1999, Natalia won a well-known national contest called the Intel Science Talent Search. Impressive, but there's more: She did it when she was only fourteen, making her the youngest-ever winner of the contest. Her project involved writing an equation to count subatomic particles called neutrinos. She compiled her research while attending a summer program at the Massachusetts Institute of Technology. What did she win? A $50,000 college scholarship, which she hopes to use at MIT.

GOOD NEWS

In 2003, 29 percent of the scientists inducted into the National Academy of Sciences were women. That's a much higher female figure than in past years, when it was only 5 to 10 percent.

Cool Quote

Our future lies with today's kids and tomorrow's space explosion.

—SALLY RIDE, astronaut

FOR MORE INFORMATION

Cool Careers for Girls in Engineering and *Cool Careers for Girls in Computers*, by Ceel Pasternak and Linda Thornburg (Impact Publications, 1999). Part of a great series that spotlights particular careers.

Girl Net: A Girl's Guide to the Internet and More, by Sarra Manning (Scholastic, 2001). Valuable Web tips and tricks for girls of all ages and levels of online knowledge.

Girls' E-Mentoring Program, www.uic.edu/orgs/gem-set. Online advice and guidance for junior-high and high-school girls interested in science or engineering; also has scholarship info.

The Math Book for Girls and Other Beings Who Count, and *The Science Book for Girls and Other Intelligent Beings,* by Valerie Wyatt (Kids Can Press, 2000 and 1997). Simple experiments and projects that connect math and science to your daily life.

Not So Wild A Dream, www.hhmi.org/dream. This site, a public service of the Howard Hughes Medical Institute, lets you see and listen to scientists, teachers, and young people who've turned their dreams into exciting careers.

Sally Ride Science Club, www.sallyrideclub.com. Created by Dr. Sally Ride, the first woman in space, for upper-elementary and middle school girls.

Super Women in Science, by Kelly Di Domenico (Second Story Press, 2003). A collection of short biographies of outstanding women.

The Technology Book for Girls and Other Advanced Beings, by Trudee Romanek (Kids Can Press, 2001). A fun look at "everyday" technology.

The Ultimate Girls' Guide to Science: From Backyard Experiments to Winning the Nobel Prize!, by Beth Caldwell Hoyt and Erica Ritter (Beyond Words, 2003). Easy experiments and lots of encouragement for any girl even remotely interested in science.

Young Women of Achievement: A Resource for Girls in Science, Math, and Technology, by Frances A. Karnes and Kristen R. Stephens (Prometheus Books, 2002). Discusses career possibilities and planning, along with stories from girls and young women who have achieved success in these fields.

BIOGRAPHIES

A to Z of Women in Science and Mathematics, by Lisa Yount (Facts on File, 1999)

Extraordinary Women Scientists, by Darlene R. Stille (Children's Book Press, 1995)

Find Where the Wind Goes: Moments From My Life, by Dr. Mae Jemison (Scholastic, 2001)

Girls Think of Everything: Stories of Ingenious Inventions by Women, and *The Sky's the Limit: Stories of Discovery by Women and Girls*, by Catherine Thimmesh (Houghton Mifflin, 2000 and 2002)

Remember the Ladies! 100 Great American Women, by Cheryl Harness (HarperCollins Juvenile Books, 2001)

Wings and Rockets: The Story of Women in Air and Space, and *Girls Who Looked Under Rocks: The Lives of Six Pioneering Naturalists*, by Jeannine Atkins (Farrar Straus & Giroux, 2003; Dawn Publications, 2000)

Women of NASA, quest.arc.nasa.gov/women/intro/html/

Chapter 8

Leave Me Alone!

What would you do if you found out that guys were writing sexually oriented graffiti about you on the stalls in the boys' bathroom at school?

This happened to Katy Lyle of Duluth, Minnesota, when she was fifteen. When she told one of the school counselors about it, it was supposedly handled, but nothing happened. Her brother was able to clean off some of the writing, but other parts were permanently etched in the metal. So Katy's family got involved, asking (sixteen times) that something be done. After six months, the school district finally had the bathroom painted, but by then the Lyles had filed a lawsuit.

Katy's experience was a form of sexual harassment. Many incidents are less serious than this, and most don't result in lawsuits, but they're all against the law.

What exactly constitutes sexual harassment? Unwelcome behavior—often at school or work—that makes you feel offended or react negatively, such as when someone:

★ Makes sexual comments, jokes, or gestures

★ Leers or whistles at you

★ Flashes or "moons" you

★ Touches, grabs, or pinches you (for example, snapping your bra strap)

★ Intentionally brushes up against you

★ Asks you about your sexual experience

★ Pressures you to engage in unwanted sexual behavior

★ Claims that you're lesbian or gay

★ Spreads sex-related rumors

★ Passes sexually explicit notes in class

★ Displays pornographic photos or drawings in public areas

★ Stalks you (follows you against your will)

Sexual harassment should not be confused with flirting, which is not offensive and usually feels good to the person receiving it. "It is the *reaction of the harassee*, not the intent of the harasser, that is important," says Nan Stein, director of the Sexual Harassment in Schools Project at the Center for Research on Women at Wellesley College. "No matter what you wear or how sexy you look, nobody has the right to sexually harass you," adds Harriet Hodgson, author of *Powerplays*, a teen guide to sexual harassment. She chose that title because "sexual harassment isn't about sex—it's about power." The harasser wants control over the victim and uses sexuality to get it.

Despite its inappropriateness, most teens report that sexual harassment "happens all the time" at their school. According to a study by the American Association of University Women (AAUW), 83 percent of teen girls in public schools have experienced some form of it (and so have 79 percent of boys); girls have also been known to harass other girls.

How "Harassment" Became a Household Word

Sexual harassment has been a problem for years, but it wasn't taken seriously until 1991, when Judge Clarence Thomas was nominated for the U.S. Supreme Court. During his confirmation process, law professor Anita Hill came forward and said he'd sexually harassed her when she worked for him at the Equal Employment Opportunity Commission (EEOC—this is the federal agency that fights discrimination in the workplace). Hill testified that Thomas constantly asked her for dates and talked to her about pornographic films. She said she'd been deeply offended by these comments but felt she couldn't complain since he was her boss and controlled her chances for advancement.

Hill's story sounded believable, and women all over the country supported her, even though Thomas said it wasn't true. He was still confirmed as a justice, but Hill's testimony had made an impact. In 1992, the Supreme Court itself ruled that if a student can prove she's been sexually harassed at school, she can sue the school. This ruling led to sixth-grader Tianna Ugarte receiving $500,000 to compensate for sexual harassment by a boy in her class, as well as other successful suits. In 1999, the Supreme Court, led by Justice Sandra Day O'Connor, ruled that schools must take responsibility for protecting students from certain "severe" forms of sexual harassment, such as if a group of boys physically threatens female peers and prevents them from using an athletic field or computer lab on a daily basis. If school administrators don't take reasonable measures to stop the harassment, or if they're basically indifferent, they can be held liable.

But let's get back to basics: Have you been sexually harassed? If so, how did you react? Maybe you hesitated to say anything because you weren't sure if it was harassment or just flirting or teasing. Perhaps you tried to laugh it off. Maybe you were afraid to protest for fear that you'd alienate the person. That's a natural reaction among girls. But when it comes to sexual harassment, the bottom line is not what the harasser says or thinks; it's how *you* feel. Even if he's clueless that he's offending you, his behavior is not okay, and there's no reason you should put up with it.

THINGS TO DO

Ask the Harasser to Stop

If someone is repeatedly harassing you and ignoring it isn't helping, the most constructive thing you can do is ask the harasser to knock it off. Describe how the behavior makes you feel or just say it bothers you. If you'd prefer, ask a friend, parent, or other adult to be there when you talk to the harasser.

When you talk to the person, it's most effective to start statements with "I," "I'll," or "I'm." If you make "you" statements, such as "You're always bothering me," the harasser may feel criticized and get defensive. But if you simply state your feelings, he'll find it hard to verbally attack you. You're not taking responsibility for his behavior; you're just expressing how it affects you.

Here are some sample "I" statements, starting with those you can use the first time you talk to the person and ending with more aggressive ones. Practice saying them out loud so you'll be ready to use them if necessary.

★ "I'm having trouble understanding what's going on here."

★ "I feel uncomfortable when you invade my personal space."

★ "I don't like being touched by people I hardly know."

★ "I am insulted by your degrading comments about women."

★ "I want you to stop sexually harassing me."

★ "If you don't stop sexually harassing me, I'll file a complaint."

If you'd rather not to confront the harasser in person, write a letter (see the sample one on page 61). Notice how the writer gives specific examples of the harasser's behavior, explains how she feels about it, and states what she wants to happen.

Document the Harassment

If the harassment doesn't stop after you've taken this step, the next strategy is to create a written record of the incidents by recording:

★ What happened?

★ When did it occur?

★ Where did it occur?

★ Were there any witnesses?

★ What did you say in response to the harassment? (Use exact words if possible.)

★ How did the harasser respond to you? (Use exact words if possible.)

★ How did you feel about the harassment?

Letter to a Harasser

Dear Ken:

I'm writing this letter to tell you that I want you to stop bothering me. This is how you are bothering me:

1. Monday, May 14. You and James whistled at me and kept me from going to class. You made rude comments about me.
2. Tuesday, May 15. You passed gross notes to me in Mr. Jacobs's class. You distracted me and I got into trouble because I didn't hear him ask me a question.
3. Wednesday, May 16. I told you to stop picking on me. You ignored what I said and made fun of me in front of your friends. That night I started getting strange phone calls from someone; I think it was you.
4. Friday, May 18. You lied about me and told your friends that we went out together when we didn't. You said I was a "hot date." That night you and your friends began driving by my house honking the horn and yelling my name. I think you are trying to ruin my reputation.

Writing this down makes me angry. You are hurting me, and I want you to stop. I want you to: (1) stop whistling at and staring at me; (2) stop calling me rude names; (3) stop acting like I want to see you outside of class; (4) stop telling lies about me; (5) stop calling me on the phone; (6) stop driving by my house; (7) leave me alone.

Michelle

—from a University of Michigan booklet called "Tune In to Your Rights"

Make a copy of your list of questions and answers (keep the original) and take it to the principal or a counselor if you're at school, or a supervisor if you're at work.

If, after documenting and reporting the harassment, it *still* doesn't stop, it's time to get more serious. Go to a person of higher authority, such as the superintendent of schools or the director of human resources at your company. You can also contact other potentially helpful organizations or people, such as your state's Department of Education, or a lawyer. Throughout this process, keep documenting the harasser's behavior and the response of the school or organization.

Help Others Stop Harassment

In addition to dealing with harassment directed at you, you can support friends and classmates who are being harassed. There is strength in numbers, and girls who band together in solidarity increase the pressure on the harasser. If you're with someone being harassed or you see harassment taking place and you feel okay defending the recipient, jump in. Even just mentioning the key words *sexual harassment* can jolt the harasser into the realization that it's not acceptable.

Real-Life Reactions

Here are some harassment scenarios. What would you have done in these situations?

Scenario: Janette was carrying groceries to her car and noticed a man standing at a nearby pay phone. As she passed him, he stopped his phone conversation, looked at her, and said, "Nice legs!" Janette ignored his comment, but as she continued walking, he followed her.
Her response: Janette turned and confronted the man, demanding to know what he was doing.

Scenario: Sonya was standing at her locker when her boyfriend, Mark, and a group of his friends approached her. When she turned to greet them, Mark cornered her against the lockers, cupping her breast in his hand. As his friends looked on in amusement, he said, "Hey, baby, I'm looking forward to Friday night."
Her response: Later, Sonya told Mark that what he did had made her uncomfortable and asked him not to do it again.

Scenario: Lisa had recently begun a new job. Since the first day, a number of male coworkers had made comments about her appearance and inquired about her sexual experience. During a lunch break, one of them put his hand on her leg and whispered, "I know what you're looking for."
Her response: Lisa spoke to another coworker about the incident. The two of them then met with their supervisor.

—courtesy of King County Sexual Assault Resource Center

Cool Quote

 No one can make you feel inferior without your consent.

—ELEANOR ROOSEVELT, first lady, humanitarian

FEMALE FIRST

NAME: **Diane Williams**

FIRST FEMALE TO: **win a lawsuit for sexual harassment from her boss**

 Williams, who'd been a public information aide at the Department of Justice in Washington, D.C., was fired in 1972. In her suit she said she'd rejected sexual advances by her boss, and pointed out that men didn't have to face these kinds of situations. In 1976, a U.S. District Court judge agreed, awarding her almost $20,000.

FOR MORE INFORMATION

Back Off: How to Confront and Stop Sexual Harassment and Harassers, by Martha Langelan (Fireside, 1993). Inspiring stories of success from girls to whole groups of women.

Everything You Need to Know About Student-on-Student Sexual Harassment, by Debbie Stanley (Rosen Publishing Group, 2000). A comprehensive guide you can probably find at the library.

"Sexual Harassment in the Schools: a Blueprint for Action," NOW Legal Defense and Education Fund, 395 Hudson St., New York, NY 10014; 212-925-6635, www.legalmomentum.org/issues/edu/blueprint.pdf. A handy tip sheet.

Teen Victim Project, National Center for Victims of Crime, www.ncvc.org/tvp/bulletins/sexualharassment. A great web site with loads of facts; even has a tip sheet on how to help a friend being harassed. Help hotline: 800-FYI-CALL.

"Tune In to Your Rights: A Guide for Teenagers About Turning Off Sexual Harassment," Programs for Educational Opportunity, 1033 School of Education Building, University of Michigan, Ann Arbor, MI 48109-1259, 313-763-9910, www.umich.edu/~eqtynet/pubs.html. A booklet for grades 7–12. $4.

Chapter 9

Know the Score

Who's playing more sports than ever, pushing the limits, breaking records, and changing perceptions about girls and women in athletics?

It's a good bet that *you* are! Opportunities for girls and women in sports have never been greater because of a landmark law called Title IX, which outlawed sex discrimination in all educational programs and activities that receive federal funding. This means that if your girls' team doesn't get new uniforms but the boys' team does, or if your team always has to practice in the old gym while the guys practice in the new one, you have grounds for complaint. (It also means boys can be cheerleaders, and that cheerleaders are supposed to perform at the same number of girls' as boys' games.)

Before Title IX came along in 1972, there were hardly any athletic scholarships for women. Now there are more than ten thousand. Girls used to be barred from many sports opportunities. Today they can join all-boy teams and compete in male-dominated sports. Thanks to Title IX, the number of girls playing high school sports increased from 294,000 (7 percent of school athletes) in 1971 to almost 2.8 million (42 percent). Still, says a report by the National Coalition for Women and Girls in Education, "Much distance remains between the current status of women and girls in sports and the ultimate goal of gender equity."

Some of that distance lies in the world of professional sports, where the money and media coverage are still focused on male sports such as football, basketball, baseball, and hockey. Fewer fans attend women's events or watch them on TV (although tennis, gymnastics, ice skating, and the Olympics in general now have more women in the spotlight). Girls' and women's teams don't have the status of boys' and men's teams, and their coaches are generally underpaid. Plus, girls in areas ranging from community softball to the professional level still experience sexism. For instance, when Angela Ruggiero, a member of the U.S. Olympic gold-medal ice hockey team, was home for a holiday break, she went to her local hockey rink to play a pick-up game. The guy at the desk told her girls weren't allowed. "Totally appalled, I let him know I was just back from Japan after winning a gold medal at the Olympic Games in Nagano," she recalls. "But all he said was "'Sorry, no exceptions.'"

Sports Figures

If you play even one sport, you know firsthand that being an athlete—either competitively or just for fun—builds your physical strength, relieves stress, and helps you stay healthy. But did you know that sports can also improve your self-esteem? Yep—studies show that female athletes are more self-reliant, get better grades, score higher on tests, are less likely to smoke, and feel better about their bodies than nonathletes. Playing sports also helps you develop skills that will come in handy in the future, such as how to be an effective team player and competitor (the majority of female business executives in one survey had played an organized sport when they were young). And according to Dr. Sylvia Rimm, author of *See Jane Win*, successful women's most mentioned, positive childhood experience is "winning in competition." Now for one final factoid: sports are just plain *fun*, according to most girls.

To sum up: *Suit* up!

THINGS TO DO

Be a Sport

You've got lots of choices when it comes to sports. If you think you'd like being on a competitive team, try basketball, soccer, volleyball, rowing, field hockey, or softball. If you like the idea of teamwork but also want to push your personal limits, consider cross country, track and field, tennis, swimming, diving, or martial arts. If you'd enjoy sports most when you're not winning or losing but just *playing*, consider hiking, skating, sailing, or bicycling. There's one more option: If after reading this chapter, you still aren't interested, why not volunteer to keep score for your favorite girls' team or write about girls' athletics for the school newspaper?

Push Yourself to New Heights

Want to beat your rival school, set a school or league record, or become an Olympian? As with any dream, it pays to set goals. Aim for achievements that are slightly out of reach, and then visualize reaching them. The trick is to break each goal into smaller "chunks," like stepping stones; that way you're focused on getting to each intermediate goal. For example, let's say you want to be most valuable player on the basketball team. Your first goal might be to score a certain amount of points per game. Then you could concentrate on winning a certain amount of games.

For inspiration, think of other girls and women who've achieved great success in sports, including Olympic-gold-medal-winning gymnast Carly Patterson and the U.S. basketball, soccer, and softball teams (2004). Golfer Annika Sorenstam, who, after becoming the world's best, went up against the men; Cristen Powell, the youngest winning female drag-racer in history; competitive skateboarder Sasha LaRochelle, 15, and tennis powerhouses Venus and Serena Williams. And there are many more!

Start a Girls' Team

Is your school lacking a girls' team in the sport you want to play? Provided that enough girls are interested, you can lobby for one. Talk to the director of the athletics department or your P.E. teacher. Consider the details: Is there a girls' league in the area? Would your team play against the boys' team? Ask that the school provide a coach, uniforms, and equipment if enough girls sign up (remember, Title IX requires schools to provide equal opportunities). If the idea gets a green light, start recruiting players and post a sign-up sheet in the locker room. Encourage all your friends and classmates to join. Play ball!

Join a Boys' Team

An all-girl team is one way to go; joining a coed team is another. If this makes sense for you, try out. Be prepared for some resistance from the boys at first. "Some boys think girls are trying to outdo them in their sport, and that's a threat," says Meghan Gagliardi, thirteen, who joined a coed soccer team in Thunder Bay, Ontario. "They're afraid you might be better than they are." As a result, they might make fun of you, not include you in the action, or make your experience so miserable that you quit. The first year Gagliardi played, she wasn't very good. "The boys teased me and had this attitude like, 'You're a girl—you shouldn't even be here!'" she says. "They would trip me, and I would think, *Why am I doing this?*"

In this kind of situation, the best tactic is to concentrate on playing the sport. When you've stuck with it for a while, teammates should begin to appreciate your determination and ability. This was certainly the case for Gagliardi, who continued for two years and steadily improved her skills. Now the same boys who snubbed her are her friends, and the team "accepts me as just another team member."

GOOD NEWS

Since 1896, when Greek marathoner Melpomene became the first woman to compete in a modern Olympics, the number of female Olympians and Olympic sports has increased dramatically. In 2004 women made up 44 percent of the Olympic athletes, and boxing was the only sport in which women couldn't compete.

FEMALE FIRSTS

NAME: **Billie Jean King**
FIRST FEMALE TO: **beat a man in a professional tennis match**

In 1973, fifty-five-year-old former tennis champion Bobby Riggs challenged King to a match. With more than thirty thousand people watching live and sixty million watching it on TV, she beat Riggs (6–4, 6–3, 6–3).

NAME: **Ashley Martin**
FIRST FEMALE TO: **play and score in an NCAA Division I football game**

Two other women had made it on to NCAA teams but hadn't actually played. Martin, playing for Jacksonville State University in 2001, kicked three successful field goals in a history-making moment that earned her a standing ovation.

Girls Can't Throw

BY MARIAH BURTON NELSON ★ Arlington, Virginia

I've heard a lot of dumb questions and comments about girls in sports. Since I'm a female athlete, I've come up with a few of my own answers—some snappy, some just smart. Try using them the next time you hear a stupid thing like . . .

"Baseball is for boys."

Is Victoria Brucker a boy? No, but Victoria, twelve, pitched in the Little League World Series. Is Julie Croteau a boy? No, but she played college baseball. Even way back in 1931, a woman named Jackie Mitchell pitched for the Chattanooga Lookouts, a men's team. (In a game against the Yankees, she struck out both Babe Ruth and Lou Gehrig.) And in the 1940s and 1950s, there was a women's professional league called the All-American Girls' Baseball League. In the 1990s, a team of women called the Colorado Silver Bullets began touring the country, playing against men.

"Football is for boys."

Then how come more than five hundred girls in five different states play high school football each year?

"Girls who play sports wish they were boys."

No, but we wish we had all the chances guys have to play sports—and all the support they get from other people. We wish that we could see women athletes on television more often. We wish there were more women coaches.

"You throw like a girl."

Gee, thanks for the compliment. Actually, there is no *female* style of throwing. Girls can throw balls just as well as boys. When girls or boys don't throw well, it's only because no one ever taught them how to do it.

"Boys are better athletes than girls."

Tell that to race car driver Lyn St. James, jockey Julie Krone, or dogsled racer Susan Butcher. Each has beaten men in dozens of races. In riflery, horseback riding, and many more sports, women and men compete equally. Female runners, swimmers, and tennis players have defeated men. It happens every day, in all sorts of sports: Sisters beat brothers; girlfriends beat boyfriends. Usually what matters is how much a person practices, not whether the person is a guy or a girl.

"Well, males are stronger than females."

Okay, there are differences. Glad you noticed. But up until junior high or so, some girls are just as strong as—or even stronger than—boys. Since most guys develop big muscles during puberty, they tend to be good at sports such as weight lifting and football. Some grow taller than girls, which helps them in volleyball and basketball. Girls, who usually are shorter and lighter and have more body fat than boys, tend to be better at horse racing, gymnastics, and cold-water swimming. But do girls try to keep boys off horses or out of the water? Of course not. It doesn't matter who's the very best at a sport, just that everyone gets a chance to play and get better.

"Boys don't like you if you beat them at sports."

Nobody likes to lose. Besides, not all guys feel that way, and why should we care about the ones who are so immature they can't stand to be beaten?

Mariah Burton Nelson's most recent book is We Are All Athletes.

The Power of Muscles

By GLORIA STEINEM ★ New York, New York

I come from a generation of women who didn't do sports. Being a cheerleader or a drum majorette was as far as our imaginations or role models could take us. Oh yes, there was also being a strutter—one of a group of girls who marched and danced and turned cartwheels in front of the high school band at football games. Did you know that big football universities actually gave strutting scholarships? That shouldn't sound any more bizarre than football scholarships, yet somehow it does.

But even winning one of those rare positions, the stuff that dreams were made of, was more about body display than about the considerable skill they required. You could forget about trying out for them if you didn't have the right face and figure, and my high school was full of girls who had learned to do back flips and twirl flaming batons, all to no avail. Winning wasn't about being the best in an objective competition or achieving a personal best, or even about becoming healthy or fit. It was about *being chosen*. That's one reason I and other women of my generation grew up believing—as many girls still do—that the most important thing about a female body is not what it does but how it looks, and that a woman should not be strong.

However, I gradually became aware of the benefits of being strong. Several of my unathletic friends had deserted me by joining gyms, becoming joggers, or discovering the pleasure of learning to yell and kick in self-defense class. Others who had young daughters described the unexpected thrill of seeing them learn to throw a ball or run with a freedom that hadn't been part of our lives in conscious memory.

The female ideal remains weak unless we organize to change it. The suffragists shed the unhealthy corsets that produced such a tiny-waisted, big-breasted look that fainting and smelling salts became routine. Instead, they brought in bloomers and bicycling. The point is: When women rebel against patriarchal standards, female muscle becomes more accepted.

I've come to believe that society's acceptance of muscular women may be one of the most important measures of change. Yes, we need progress everywhere, but an increase in our physical strength could have more impact on the everyday lives of most women than the occasional role model in the boardroom or in the White House. Each of us must have our own strength.

Gloria Steinem is one of the most celebrated leaders of the women's movement and a cofounder of Ms. magazine.

Cool Quote

I am a pioneer, and sports is my frontier. . . . I'm muscular, but that strength and endurance enhances, not diminishes, my femininity. I can wear six-inch nails and one-legged bodysuits and set world records. And leave a lot of men in the dust.

—FLORENCE GRIFFITH-JOYNER, sprinter

Cool Quote

 Athletes don't go through that whole thing about worrying how they look; they just want to be strong, and self-confidence is the result.

—KAREN LUNDGREN, adventure racer

FOR MORE INFORMATION

Anything You Can Do . . . New Sports Heroes for Girls by Doreen Greenberg (Wish Publishing), a series of in-depth books on athletes including swimmer Jenny Thompson, fencer Sharon Monplaisir, and others.

Game Face: What Does a Female Athlete Look Like?, by Jane Gottsman (Random House Trade Paperbacks, 2003). A colorful, awe-inspiring celebration of female athletes.

Girl Wise, www.melpomene.org/girlwise/PhysicalActivity/PhysicalActivity.htm, sponsored by the Melponene Institute. This site highlights girls' achievements and provides health tips.

Go Girl Go, www.womenssportsfoundation.org/cgi-bin/iowa/sports/ggg. This site, sponsored by the Women's Sports Foundation, covers all kinds of sports topics and offers profiles of athletes.

National Girls & Women in Sports Day, www.aahperd.org/ngwsdcentral. News about this annual event, Title IX, what's going on in your local area, and lots more.

National Women's Law Center, www.nwlc.org. Check this site for the latest Title IX- and other rights-related legislation, or if you need guidance on dealing with an unfair sports situation at your school.

The Right Moves: A Girl's Guide to Getting Fit and Feeling Good, by Tina Schwager and Michele Schuerger (Free Spirit, 1998). Easy, entertaining reading on fitness, diet, and general health.

Throw Like a Girl: Discovering the Body, Mind and Spirit of the Athlete in You, by Shelley Frost and Ann Troussieux (Beyond Words, 2000)

You Go Girl!, by Ariel Jennifer Jones (Andrews McMeel, 2000). Stories and reflections from accomplished women athletes.

Our Society

✳ ✳ ✳ ✳ ✳ ✳ ✳ ✳ ✳ ✳ ✳ ✳ ✳ ✳

Chapter 10

Media Darling

Suppose you're an alien who's just landed on Earth somewhere in the United States. Wanting to find out what humans are like, you turn on a TV, listen to the radio, read some magazines, and go to some movies. You conclude that males are the dominant figures, leaders, and "experts" in most areas. Females, it seems, aren't particularly smart, and they're primarily concerned with how they look.

Of course your conclusions wouldn't be accurate. The content of America's TV shows, songs, magazine articles, and movies (as well as advertising, which is discussed in Chapter 13) doesn't reflect women's and girls' reality.

The good news is that in the past few years, there have been improvements in some areas, such as in children's television. For example, according to Children Now, there are just as many female TV and movie characters as male characters who rely on themselves to reach goals and solve problems. However, there's still plenty of room for improvement. For example, 90 percent of the stars of children's TV programs are still male. And Girls Incorporated is not impressed with the roles of the few females. Its assessment: "Girls on TV are weak followers who need boys to make their decisions; popular only if they are beautiful, thin, weak, compliant, and not too bright." In addition, very few prime-time shows have a plot about a girl's academic pursuits or career plans. And women still commonly hold traditional or stereotypical roles (secretaries, housewives, beauty objects).

TV isn't the only form of media that needs improvement. Take product packaging, for instance. Next time you're at the grocery store, look at the images on labels and boxes. A survey by the Guerilla Girls (see Chapter 14) of cereal boxes revealed that twenty out of twenty feature male characters (such as the bee on Honey Nut Cheerios and the chimp on Coco Krispies). Girls eat cereal too, and they also make buying decisions. Where are the female cereal mascots?

Behind the Media

Part of the reason for all of this inequity is that women aren't well represented *working in* the media. According to the American Society of Newspaper Editors, they make up only 37 percent of reporters at daily newspapers. They're just 24 percent of television writers, directors, and producers. And the major network news shows have women as on-air experts only 13 percent of the time (even in stories about women or girls).

Attention writers, producers, TV networks, and other contributors to popular culture: Pay attention to how you're portraying girls and women and what you can do to be more inclusive. There's no law that the media has to be fair or accurate, but there's a good reason for it to be both: Women and girls are more than half of the population and half of all media consumers!

THINGS TO DO ———

Watch the News

One key to dealing with the media is awareness. "Once girls understand the effects of the culture on their lives, they can fight back," says Mary Pipher, author of *Reviving Ophelia.* In this case, you can raise your awareness by evaluating the news on its inclusion and portrayal of women and girls. Here are tip-offs that coverage is biased, from Fairness and Accuracy in Reporting (FAIR):

★ The important news stories are reported by men.

★ News is reported from a male perspective (for example, only covering how men are affected).

★ Very few women, but loads of men, are interviewed or quoted as "experts."

★ Different standards are used for women and men. For example, sports announcers often comment on women's hairstyles or other physical traits but seldom call attention to how men look.

★ There are stereotypes (for example, a story about Welfare spotlighting only black women, when plenty of white men are also on Welfare).

When you see news you feel is biased (or impressively fair), get the news organization's address (see page 79) and write a letter. Include the name of the story, author or reporter, and date; also include your name, address, and phone number. Send to "Letters to the Editor" if it's a newspaper or magazine, or "Manager" if it's a TV or radio station.

Rate TV Shows on Gender Bias and Stereotypes

Make copies of this questionnaire, fill them out, and send them to the networks that air the shows (see page 79 for contact information).

TV SHOW DATA SHEET

Name of show_____

Lead female character's name_____

Her occupation or interests _____

Is her appearance frequently discussed?   Y   N

Her personality traits _____

Her problems and challenges_____

Lead male character's name_____

His occupation or interests _____

Is his appearance frequently discussed?   Y   N

His personality traits_____

His problems and challenges _____

Based on these answers, rate each of the shows on a scale of 1 to 10 for gender bias and stereotyping (1 is no bias; 10 is major bias).

Your best-rated show_____ Rating_____

Your worst-rated show_____ Rating_____

Grow a Phone Tree

Girls Incorporated has a program called Girls Recast TV that helps its members see how the media affects them. One of its projects is to start a phone tree—a network of girls who respond to media bias.

To start a tree, write down the names of two or more friends you'll contact when you see an offensive media incident. Ask each friend to write down two or more names of people *they'll* call, and have those people ask for two more names apiece, and so on to form other "branches." When one of you sees something on TV that you want to protest (or applaud), immediately call your branches and ask them to call theirs so you can all watch and evaluate it. Then have everyone write or call the network. You can make this process even simpler by having everyone assemble a media-monitoring kit to keep near the TV: a pen, stationery, envelopes, stamps, and media organization contact information (and of course your phone tree list). *Voila*, your collective voice comes across loud and clear! The more protests the network gets, the less likely it will be to rebroadcast the show or air a similar one.

Listen to Lyrics

"I have nothing against different types of music, but I have a little problem with rap music," says Anna Folman of Columbus, Ohio. "Why do rappers call women mean, nasty names?" Good question. Because while free-speech laws say that bands should be able to sing about whatever they want, anti-female lyrics help legitimize contempt for women and violence against them. If the words to a song offend you, write to the company that produced the CD (the address should be on the inside flap of the liner). Circle or highlight the lyrics. Tell the company why you find them offensive, and that you don't plan to buy any more of the group's CDs.

FEMALE FIRST

NAME: **Katie Couric**

FIRST FEMALE TO: **be highest-compensated anchor (ever!)**

Couric demonstrated that she could be "the serious news interviewer in one segment, talking to senators or the president, and be Peter Pan in the next segment," according to the president of NBC. This made her more valuable than her colleagues, who were earning $8-12 million per year. Her annual earnings? $60 million.

How to Get the Media's Ear

Here's how to reach some of America's major media organizations:

ABC
500 South Buena Vista Street
Burbank, CA 91521-4551
818-460-7477
www.abc.com

CNN
www.cnn.com

Fox Broadcasting Company
P.O. Box 900
Beverly Hills, CA 90213
www.fox.com

ABC News
7 West 66th Street
New York, NY 10023
Audience Relations: 212-456-7777
www.abcnews.com

MSNBC
www.msnbc.com

CBS News
555 West 57th Street
New York, NY 10019
212-975-4114
www.cbs.com

NBC
30 Rockefeller Plaza
New York, NY 10112
www.nbc.com

CBS Television Network
51 West 52nd Street
New York, NY 10019
212-975-4321
www.cbs.com

MTV
1515 Broadway
New York, NY 10036
212-258-8000
www.mtv.com

USA Today
www.usatoday.com

For contact information not shown here, try a search engine such as Google, or check with a reference librarian.

One-Girl Revolution

Animated and liberated, Lisa Simpson wages a one-girl revolution against cartoonland patriarchy every week on Fox TV's *The Simpsons*, created by Matt Groening. Whether she's marching for gay rights, subverting Thanksgiving with a tribute to forgotten foremothers, or demanding equal pay for equal work during household chores, Lisa's personal is intensely political. She told *Ms.* that role models such as Simone de Beauvoir and George Eliot fueled her feminism, as did "the off chance that my father, Homer, and my brother, Bart—much as I love them—represent a fair cross section of American men." In her crusade against sexism, Lisa recently took on the makers of the talking Malibu Stacy doll—which exclaims, "I wish they taught shopping in school." She marketed her own Lisa Lionheart doll, who tells girls, "Trust in yourself and you can achieve anything!" Despite her desire to one day be chief justice or president of the United States, Lisa says, "I imagine that in twenty years—as during the past five seasons—I shall find myself still in the second grade at Springfield Elementary." But to her live-action sisters, she urges: "Go forth to third grade! And beyond! I'm counting on you."

—from *Ms.* magazine

FOR MORE INFORMATION

Everything You Need to Know About Media Violence, by Kathy Edgar (Rosen Publishing Group, 1998). A good starting point for info on this subject.

Girls, Women + Media Project, *www.mediaandwomen.org.* Fact packed and full of good ideas to make you media literate.

Media Watch, *www.mediawatch.org* (see page 20 in Chapter 2).

Mind on the Media, 710 St. Olaf Ave., Suite 200, Northfield, MN 55057; *www.motm.org.* This organization launched by *New Moon* sponsors "Turn Beauty Inside Out Day" and other effective pro-girl campaigns.

Teen Health and the Media, depts.washington.edu/thmedia. An informative site (see the news articles, in particular) sponsored by the Washington State Department of Health advocating media literacy.

Third Wave Foundation "I Spy Sexism" campaign, *www.thirdwavefoundation.org/programs/i_spy_sexism.html.* Has a printable postcard you can sign and send to offenders.

Chapter 11

The "Old Boys' Club"

What's the *one* symbolic thing that would most signify equality for America's girls and women?

If you're like many girls and women, you answered "A female president."

That would be a symbolic victory, and a natural one after decades of steady progress for women in elected office (see the timeline on pages x–xi). When will America embrace a female leader?

While the White House would be a major win, the office of the president is only one target. There's also Congress, as well as state and local governments. Women make up only 15 percent of Congress and 23 percent of state legislatures. It's still mainly guys (the Senate is known as "The Old Boys' Club") who write, debate, and pass the laws—including laws that mainly affect women.

Why aren't there more women in the U.S. government? According to a group called the White House Project, whose goal is to elect a female president, only 43 percent of young women say they'd want to run for office, and that's partly because they don't find the Old Boy climate attractive. Another limiting factor is that women are rarely seen in leadership roles, such as on TV political-debate shows. The White House Project notes: "There are women in positions of great power and authority in our country, but they are not invited guests on the Sunday shows. . . . The public needs to see women who are in positions of power, and the country needs to hear what women have to say." This is true not only at the national level but in each state and local community.

The Power of the Women's Vote

Leadership is important, but voting is equally crucial. Did you know that there are *ten million* more American women registered to vote than men? That's right—women are 53 percent—the *majority*—of America's voters. This means they have the ability to influence elections profoundly. The problem is some female voters don't vote for candidates who support women's rights, or they don't vote at all, perhaps because they don't realize its importance. Some married women simply vote the same way their husbands do. And other women, such as working single moms, are so focused on trying to make it through each day that voting seems like a hardship.

Before women won the right to vote in 1920, many men were opposed to sharing this privelage with the opposite sex.

It's simple: When the majority of women vote for candidates and issues that support women and girls, we'll have an equal society. Equal representation isn't just a right and a privilege, it's a *duty*. "The most important thing for feminism is that young people vote," says actor Camryn Manheim.

Achieving Balance

It may seem obvious, but it's worth considering: More female legislators translate into better quality of life for women and girls. Male politicians can advocate for female concerns, and many do. But according to the Center for the American Woman in Politics, it's the female officeholders who are more likely to push for policies and laws supporting women's rights. Want proof? The states with the highest percentage of female legislators also have the smallest "gender pay gap." In addition, women come up with problem-solving approaches that complement men's; women are known for being inclusive and gathering input before making decisions.

Predominantly male leadership is not only a handicap, it can have consequences for *both* genders. For instance, what happens when a 95-percent-male governing body debates family leave (the concept of requiring companies to let workers take time off to care for kids or aging parents)? For the most part, these men aren't the ones trying to balance work with taking care of their families, so they may not realize why the law makes so much sense. Now imagine the legislation being debated by a group of half women and half men. It stands a chance.

"Women populate half the democracy; we should occupy half the positions of leadership—both for gender equity and because women, a natural resource, should be mined for energy," says Marie Wilson, author of *Closing the Leadership Gap: Why Women Can and Must Help Run the World*. "Our future depends on the leadership of women—not to replace men, but to transform our options alongside them."

THINGS TO DO ———————

Join a Political Organization

Okay, you're too young to vote, but you can still be an effective force for issues that matter to you. Many activist organizations have teen members who do everything *but* vote—they help support laws, organize rallies, and work to inform the public about campaigns. Joining an organization can be a rewarding because groups generally get more attention than individuals. In fact, much of the recent progress in women's rights is thanks to activist groups, whose members leaflet, picket, protest, hold marches, and organize letter-writing campaigns.

Here are three organizations working fervently to advance women's rights. Find out what they do and see if they feel like a fit.

Feminist Majority Foundation, 1600 Wilson Blvd., Suite 801, Arlington, VA 22209, 703-522-2214, www.feminist.org.

National Organization for Women, 733 15th St. NW, 2nd Floor, Washington, DC 20005; 202-785-8669, www.now.org.

Third Wave Foundation, 511 West 25th St., Suite 301, New York, NY 10001; 212-675-0700, www.thirdwavefoundation.org.

Help a Female Candidate

Think government might be the place for you? Volunteering for a woman running for office is an up-close way to check out the world of politics. You'll be gathering valuable information while supplying something equally valuable: As

LOOK GUYS... WHY DON'T WE JUST SAY THAT ALL MEN ARE CREATED EQUAL... AND LET THE LITTLE LADIES LOOK OUT FOR THEMSELVES?

U.S. Representative Lynn Woolsey attests, "The hard work and dedication of truly committed individuals is one of the main reasons I am in Congress today."

How do you find a candidate to assist? If this is an election year (which occurs every two years), read the newspaper or watch the local news to see who's mentioned, or call city hall and ask for the names and phone numbers of local female candidates. Call their campaign offices or do some research to find out what issues they support. If a candidate cares about women's rights and other things you support, offer to stuff envelopes, answer phones, hand out brochures—whatever they need.

Help Get Young Women Registered to Vote

In the 2004 presidential election, a record number of people under age 30 voted—approximately 20.9 million—the highest turnout for this age group since 1972. One contributor to this result was the music group the Dixie Chicks, which teamed up with Rock the Vote (www.rockthevote.com) in a campaign called "Chicks Rock, Chicks Vote!" You can add to this initial success by helping more young women (and men) get motivated and registered to vote. It's more important than ever to convince women that their votes matter and to help them understand how electing particular candidates will impact their lives.

Learn How to Lead

"Never before have there been so many well-educated young women who could grab the controls," notes Representative Pat Schroeder in *Sisterhood is Forever*. If you think you might be one of these people (and the country needs *lots* of them), look into a program such as Girls State, which is run by the American Legion Auxiliary. In this week-long national summer program, you play the role of a lawmaker and take part in legislative sessions and debates; you also get an opportunity to meet real lawmakers. To find a leadership program, visit the White House Project's Web site (see page 92).

Tell Your Representatives What You Think

Even if you don't plan to become a governor or senator, you can still help women by voicing your opinions to your reps in Congress and locally. Government leaders must answer to the people in their district, including those your age, or they won't get reelected. Let's say you see on TV that next week, Congress plans to vote on whether to cut funding for victims of domestic violence. *That's* the time to tell your representatives a piece of your mind. For more general concerns, the month of December, before the new legislative session begins and when things have slowed down, is an especially good time to make contact. If you don't know your representatives or senators' names, you can find them on *www.house.gov/writerep* and *www.senate.gov*, which also provide e-mail addresses.

Here's the address to use for sending mail to your representatives:

The Honorable [first and last name]
House of Representatives
Washington, DC 20515

And for your senator:

The Honorable [first and last name]
United States Senate
Washington, DC 20510

So you're ready to sound off to your representative. What do you say? *The Kid's Guide to Social Action* suggests:

★ Immediately state the purpose of the letter.

★ Discuss only one issue in each letter.

★ If you're writing about a certain bill, include its number and name.

★ Keep the letter short—a few paragraphs at the most.

★ If you disagree with the rep, explain that in a polite way; never be rude or threatening.

★ If possible, mention something positive that the rep has done. This could make her or him more receptive to your suggestion.

★ Don't apologize for taking up the official's time—communicating with constituents is part of her or his job.

★ If for some reason you contact a representative other than your own, send a copy to your rep (this is considered good manners).

★ Include your return address so the legislator can write back.

A Quick Quiz: Women in Government

Test your knowledge! Make a copy of this page or write your answers on a separate sheet of paper.

1. Of the 100 senators and 535 representatives in the U.S. Congress in 2005, how many were women?
    a. 11   b. 28   c. 79   d. 200

2. How many minority women are in Congress?
    a. 19   b. 38   c. 61   d. 72

3. Who was the first woman to lead her party in Congress?
    a. Martha Hughes Cannon in 1896   b. Rebecca Latimer Felton in 1922
    c. Christine Todd Whitman in 1997   d. Nancy Pelosi in 2003

4. As a group, women and men see things significantly differently (there's a gender gap) in which of these areas?
    a. Voting   b. Party identification   c. Evaluations of presidents' records
    d. All of the above

5. 1992 was called "The Year of the Woman." Why?
    a. 1991 was the "The Year of the Man."
    b. The first female governor was elected.
    c. A relatively large number of women were voted into office
    d. Why *not?*

6. Which country has the highest percentage of women in its main legislative assembly?
    a. Norway   b. Sweden   c. Spain   d. The United States

From Girl to Governor

By ANN RICHARDS ★ former governor of Texas

When I was a girl taking "vocational preference" tests, I never saw the career choice of "politician" on any of them. That's because the girls were given different tests than the boys, so the choices were predictably limited: if our answers indicated an interest in people or their problems, the choice was something like social worker or nurse, not politician. But what better way is there to serve people than to go into public service?

I got interested in politics in high school, when I attended Girls State, a camplike workshop on local government, and Girls Nation, the Washington counterpart. After high school I worked in a volunteer capacity in numerous local election campaigns. I had never thought nor hoped to run for office myself. Women were not allowed roles of responsibility beyond licking stamps or making copies, no matter how much experience or education we had. It was my husband who insisted that we alter our lifestyle and invest time and money in my pursuit of public office. I was elected county commissioner in Travis County in 1976 and eventually became governor in 1990.

Many people in government service whom I visited when I was county commissioner said they had never been called on by a government official before. They couldn't believe I was truly interested in their agency or department. Some women fear that they lack experience, but our interest and willingness to give of ourselves far surpasses the male officeholders that have gone before us.

An increasing number of women are finding that politics offers us an opportunity to act on what we think. We've decided to *do* rather than to *observe*. The contributions of women in government have figured significantly in making the United States a better place. For example, I and other women officeholders have worked to make government inclusive rather than exclusive. We have worked to bring in those citizens who have been previously left out of the power structure: men and women from all walks of life and viewpoints.

Now it's up to young women and girls to seize new leadership opportunities. Then when the question is raised (as it was in my campaign) if a woman can be governor (or city council member, or mayor, or president), the answer will be "Why not?"

A Girl's Place Is in the House

By AMANDA KELLER, thirteen ★ Bethesda, Maryland

My cousin Lisa, who's into politics, has always wanted me to be a politician. But to me, the whole government process seemed too complicated. I hardly knew there *was* a House of Representatives or a Senate, much less what they did. I basically thought the president did everything. So Lisa arranged for me to hang around with Representative Anna Eschoo on Take Our Daughters to Work Day.*

When I got to Anna's office in Washington, one of her assistants showed me how things worked. Then Anna had a meeting, and I watched from where the public sits. Afterward, she invited me to go down on the floor, where the representatives were. And then she had to go up in the Speaker's chair, so I went, too! It was pretty cool. I really enjoyed it, and it was good to see how everything worked.

That was my one big experience with government, and it made me see that there's more to politics than just the presidency. Being on the floor and seeing what Anna did made me realize that I could do it, too, and use the position to have an impact on women's rights. It inspired me to get into politics—in fact, it made me want to maybe go a step *higher*, to something even more exciting, like running for the Senate or the vice presidency.

*Now called Take Our Daughters and Sons to Work Day

GOOD NEWS

Some state governments are making progress at closing their numbers gaps between women and men. In Washington state, there are almost as many female legislators as there are male. Arizona, Colorado, Connecticut, Minnesota, and Vermont have also made gains.

FEMALE FIRSTS

NAMES: **Tarja Halonen and Anneli Jaatteeenmaki**

FIRST FEMALES TO: **hold both the offices of president and prime minister (Finland)**

 Finland gave women the right to vote before any other European country, in 1906. Tarja Halonen was elected president in 2000. Then, in 2003, Jaatteeenmaki's political party became the dominant party in Parliament (a governing body that's 40 percent female).

NAME: **Wilma Mankiller**

FIRST FEMALE TO: **be elected chief of the Cherokee Nation of Oklahoma**

In the late 1950, Mankiller started doing volunteer work in the local Cherokee community, directed a Native American youth center, and cofounded an alternative school. All of this helped prepare her to lead the Cherokee Nation, which she did from 1985 to 1995. She's credited with creating better health care services and prospects for education, training, and employment for her people.

Cool Quotes

 Never doubt that a small group of thoughtful, concerned citizens can change the world. Indeed, it is the only thing that ever has.

—MARGARET MEAD, anthropologist

Some leaders are born women.

—GERALDINE FERRARO, first female candidate for vice president

FOR MORE INFORMATION

Any Girl Can Rule the World, by Susan M. Brooks (Fairview, 1998) An information-packed handbook.

Can a Girl Run for President? by Christine Harvey (Intrinsic, 2000). If you envision yourself in a leadership role, here's an inspiring read.

Extraordinary Women in Politics, by Charles Gulotta (Children's Book Press, 1999). Profiles 55 women from both the past and the present.

GenderGap.com, www.gendergap.com. Details and statistics on American women in government (past and present).

Girls and Young Women Leading the Way, by Frances A. Karnes and Suzanne M. Bean (Free Spirit, 1993). Stories about activists along with with practical tips.

Girl Scouts of the USA, 420 Fifth Avenue, New York, NY 10018, 800-478-7248 or 212-852-8000; www.girlscouts.org. Girl Scout organizations are a good place to hone leadership skills.

Girls Matter, www.girlsmatter.com. The goal of this site is to "enable school-age young women to grow into active political participants."

Girls' Pipeline to Power, www.girlspipeline.org. Created by the Patriot's Trail Girl Scout Council; lots of activities and links to explore.

Iron Jawed Angels (HBO, 2004). This movie chronicles the struggle to attain voting rights for women.

The Kids' Guide to Social Action, by Barbara Lewis (Free Spirit, 1998). The ABCs of being an activist.

Rabble Rousers (Dutton, 2003) and *Remember the Ladies* (HarperCollins, 2001), by Cheryl Harness. Two information-packed biography collections.

The White House Project, GirlZone page, www.thewhitehouseproject.org/old_site/GirlZone/home_page.html, 110 Wall St., second floor, New York, NY 10005; (212) 785-6001. A national, nonpartisan organization committed to getting a woman into the White House. For a list of leadership programs for high-school girls, see www.thewhitehouseproject.org/become_leader/Leadership_training_front_page.htm.

Women's Voices. Women's Vote. www.wvwv.org. This site is dedicated to increasing the number of women voters.

Chapter 12

Spread the Word

Peace on Earth, goodwill toward men.

What's wrong with this phrase?

You guessed it: Women are absent. Some people would argue that *men* technically means *men and women*, but a more inclusive version is *Peace on Earth, goodwill toward all.*

Why is this little detail so important? Because language causes people to conjure up images in their heads. Male-centered language makes children picture *just males* in the same way that female-centered language makes them picture *just females*. Words and phrases such as *cameraman* and *Every man for himself* make women and girls seem insignificant. And language that excludes part of a population also has a negative impact on that group's collective self-image. It makes sense . . . How interested are *you* in something that doesn't sound applicable to you? "My science book talks about how man evolved," says Bridget Shanahan, thirteen, of Mokena, Illinois. "Didn't women evolve, too?"

While pronouns are one concern, feminists have other beefs with the English language, notably about vocabulary. Hundreds of English words referring to females have negative connotations, such as *sissy*, which is derived from *sister*; and sexual connotations, such as *slut*. By contrast, there aren't many derogatory words referring to males, and those that exist don't have the same negative punch.

What's in a Name?

Another issue is the ages-old tradition of women being labeled by their marital status (Miss or Mrs., which stand for *mistress of*), while men are simply *Mr.*, whether they're single or married. In the 1970s, women's rights supporters came up with *Ms.* as an equivalent to Mr., but it still seems to infer *Miss*.

You may also be wondering why, when a woman gets married, she usually changes her last name to her husband's. Well, It's an ancient tradition. Women used to be thought of as their husbands' property, and they gave up their names to reflect that. American women are obviously no longer considered possessions, but most brides still take their husbands' names (while some switch to a combination of their husband's and their name). Some brides are aware that the tradition is sexist, but for various and totally valid reasons—such not wanting to burden their children with long, hyphenated last names—they go along with the custom. Other women choose to keep their maiden names. Some couples hyphenate their two last names to make a new one, while others create a different last name altogether. The options aren't great, but at least they exist.

The Evolution of English

English is changing according to the way people use it every day. For example, when women and girls started using *herstory* as a complement to *history*, it became so common that it was added to the dictionary. You can probably think of other new words and phrases that now roll off of people's tongues, such as *gender-neutral, people of color*, and *physically challenged*. In addition, a study (Cronin & Jreisat) has found that high-school freshman are more likely to use nonsexist language than seniors. This indicates that each successive generation could be helping to stamp out sexist language.

THINGS TO DO ————————————

See for Yourself!

Do an experiment to see if the studies about how people form mental pictures based on language are right. Compile a list of sexist words and phrases (plus pronouns like *his*) that you've read or heard in conversations. Write a one-page story (fiction or nonfiction) that weaves the biased words into your plot. Then write the same story, substituting gender-neutral words and phrases. When you're finished, read each story to a different friend and see if the one who heard the biased story pictured more males than the one who heard the gender-neutral story. Repeat this with two more people, and then share the results with them all.

Expand Your Vocabulary

Pay attention to how you use pronouns and try to be gender neutral. Let's say you're writing a story about otters; instead of using *his* and *him* for all the

What's the Word?

Do you use any of the words and phrases in the left column? Try the alternatives in the right column.

Biased Word or Phrase	Acceptable Substitute
suffragette	suffragist
foreman	supervisor
waitress	waiter, server
landlord	building owner
majorette	major
mailman	letter carrier
chairman	chairperson or chair
policeman, fireman	police officer, firefighter
salesman	sales representative, salesperson
housewife	homemaker
woman professor	professor
cleaning lady	cleaner
stewardess	flight attendant
workmanship	artisanship
girl*	woman
lady**	woman
manmade	synthetic, manufactured
manning	staffing, running
layman	layperson, nonexpert
To each his own	To each one's own
Every dog has his day.	Every dog has its day.
She's a tomboy.	She's adventurous.
Paul's the best man for the job.	Paul's the best person for the job.
(In a letter) Dear sirs; Gentlemen	To whom it may concern, Dear [name of person], Dear [name of organization], Greetings, Hello

* *Girl* is often used to refer to women, implying immaturity. A girl is technically a female younger than about age 16.

**Lady is the equivalent to *gentleman* but connotes a weak, unremarkable person as opposed to a strong, capable one.

animals, make some of them female. If you'd normally say something like *Every kid for himself,* add *or herself.* If you find that it's too awkward to repeatedly say *his or her,* alternate the two pronouns. For example, you could refer to a generic person as *she* in one paragraph and *he* in the next (as this book does).

Enlighten Your Parents

If you start upgrading your language, your parents, friends, and teachers may, too. Or they may not . . . in which case, feel free to educate them, provided they're open to feedback. Mention how studies show that language affects the way people picture things in their minds. If the person belittling the idea is a guy, ask

Linguistic Losers

Did you notice that sexist language was unfair way before you ever read this chapter? Good job. So did these girls—here are some of their pet peeves:

★ "Why is it that when a woman doesn't get married she is called an 'old maid' and when a man doesn't get married he is called an 'eligible bachelor'?"

—Lydia Leinsdorf, New York, New York

★ "There is a bank in my area named Young Men's Savings and Loan. I think it's very sexist because women get loans, earn money, and use banks just like men do. The name should be Young People's Savings and Loan."

—Keeley McGroarty, Pitman, New Jersey

★ "How come in collegiate sports at the University of Texas they call the women's team Lady Longhorns and the men's team is just Texas or University of Texas? Why not the U.T. women's team and the U.T. men's team?"

—Chloe McCoy, nine, Austin, Texas

★ "A few days ago I had some Campbell's soup. On the back it said, 'This soup has what it takes to handle a hungry man.' I was so mad!"

—Sara Beth Behmerwohld, nine, San Juan Capistrano, California

★ "All the construction signs say MEN AT WORK. And I saw *women*."

—JeriAnn Miller, eleven, Marshall, Minnesota

—from *New Moon: The Magazine for Girls and Their Dreams*

how he'd feel if *she* and *woman* were always used to describe both men and women. It's gratifying to see people's reactions when they understand what it's like to be excluded by language.

FEMALE FIRSTS

NAME: **Lucy Stone**
FIRST FEMALE TO: **publicly protest female name changing**

In 1855, Stone's boyfriend, Henry Blackwell, proposed. She accepted but decided to keep her name because it was "the symbol of my identity and must not be lost." After the wedding she called herself "Mrs. Stone." She also wrote a marriage agreement that said she and Blackwell would be equal partners.

NAME: **Neil Popović**
FIRST MALE TO: **publicly protest female name changing**

Popović tried to change HIS last name to hers (they added his name as a second middle name). He had a tough time getting the Department of Motor Vehicles (DMV) and Internal Revenue Service (IRS) to change the name on his driver's license and tax records. But he thought it was worth the effort because it raised people's awareness of the outdated custom. "You see, even if taking my wife's name is just a tiny blip on the radar screen of social evolution," he wrote in Ms. magazine, it is still a thought-provoking act."

GOOD NEWS

As ordered by its state legislature, Minnesota removed all traces of gender bias from the wording of its laws. Editors worked for a two-year period, changing the word HIS ten thousand times and HE six thousand times.

Cool Quote

 **An actress can only play a woman. I'm an actor; I can play anything.**

—WHOOPI GOLDBERG, actor, activist

FOR MORE INFORMATION

The Bias-Free Word Finder: A Dictionary of Nondiscriminatory Language, by Rosalie Maggio (Beacon Press, 1992)

Chapter 13

Selling Us Short

"You need our products!"

That's what companies want you to believe after being exposed to their TV and radio commercials, plus ads in magazines and newspapers, on shopping carts, buses, and billboards, and on the Internet. The money advertisers spend to run ads is powerful. TV shows have even been *invented* to complement ads (for instance, "soap operas" were created so detergent manufacturers could sell to women at home). What does all of this have to do with sexism? Advertising is full of images of perfect-looking models (the companies want you to think their products will make you perfect, too). And in addition to making you feel insecure, it often reinforces sexist stereotypes.

Magazine Ads

The next time you're at a newsstand, take a closer look at the ads in some women's magazines. While a few show people who look real, you're likely to find yourself in a sea of nearly nude models and flawless faces—page after page emphasizing women's bodies over their brains. There are shots of women with their heads cut off by the top of the page, which implies that how the woman looks is more important than what she thinks. Close-up shots of thighs, breasts, lips, legs, and hips convey obsession with individual body parts. Pictures of models who look afraid, as if they've have been abused or are about to be hit, women posed like little girls, and young girls presented as grown-up sex objects all give the impression that females are powerless, immature, and mainly valuable as beauty objects.

Magazine advertising also has a way of creeping into magazine *articles*. Ever wonder why there are so many stories about putting on makeup and choosing a shampoo? An advertiser may agree to run an ad if the magazine includes an article (often positioned physically near the ad) that reinforces the need for its product. Sneaky. And how about some articles about things that really matter? "We don't need advice on how to firm our thighs," says Media Watch. "We need substantive articles."

TV Commercials

If you're an average teen, you see more than *forty thousand* TV ads each year. Yikes! Americans are bombarded with commercials featuring images of thin, bikini-clad young women flocking around beer-drinking men, and models flipping back shiny hair or proudly exhibiting glowing skin. In addition, ads' voiceovers (those media "voices of authority") are 75 percent male; including for ads for products being advertised to women and showing only female models, according to the Screen Actors' Guild.

If you think all those TV spots may affect how you see yourself and the world, you're right. A study by Duane Hargreaves found that TV commercials showing perfect-looking girls and women impact girls' confidence and make them feel less satisfied with their bodies.

A law called the Communications Act of 1934 required television to focus on what the public wants and needs, and to provide more sources of funding for TV shows (which helps alleviate the reliance on advertising). While the American Psychological Association has advocated a return to the philosophy of this law, consumer activism is a better bet for getting advertisers to change. Advertising is powerful, but so is your opinion, because companies want your business. "Women have such tremendous power as consumers that when a woman writes a letter to a magazine—objecting, for example, to some ad's portrayals of women—that letter is counted as representing *ten thousand readers*," explains author Naomi Wolf, in *Fire with Fire: The New Female Power and How to Use It*. That's right; you've got power too.

THINGS TO DO

Provide Advertisers with Feedback

The next time you see a TV commercial or ad that portrays women in a negative way, tell the company (call 1-800-555-1212 to get its 800 number), the TV station running the ad (see page 79 for networks' addresses), or the magazine in which it appeared. If you find an ad that portrays women in a *positive* way, register your approval; the company will appreciate that, too. Chances are you won't be the only person reacting to a particular ad, and if others are saying what you're saying, look out. . . . companies have yanked offensive ads and even gone so far as to design entirely new ad campaigns.

Attention, All You Advertisers!

A group of girls participating in "Turn Beauty Inside Out Day," an event sponsored by Mind on the Media (see page 81), met with advertising industry executives to voice their concerns about how ads portray women and girls. The girls gave the executives this list of "best practices."

1. Don't just think about how it's going to affect the target audience but about everybody who's going to see the ad (girls, boys, and kids, for example).

2. Don't assume that the people who'll see the ad are "mindless droids." Their opinions really matter.

3. Only show women and girls when you need them in order to sell the product.

4. Don't cut up body parts . . . show the woman as a whole person.

5. Use a variety of body sizes and shapes in your ads.

6. We need more diversity in ads; use more people of color.

7. Try to sell the product without using sex or making other provocative suggestions.

8. Ads lower girls' self-esteem and make girls depressed. Instead, they should encourage and build self-esteem.

9. Use the body in an appropriate way in your ads; stop dressing women in skimpy (or no) clothes.

10. Beware of the "Girlcaught" (for info, visit www.mindonthemedia.org). Girls are going to catch the bad ads and call companies on them.

Forward Bad Ads to MS.

Want to call attention to a particularly awful, sexist ad? Send it to the editors of *Ms.*, who choose the worst ones to feature on the magazine's back cover. Include the whole page on which the ad appears, the name and date of the publication, and your name and address. Send it to: "No Comment," *Ms.*, 433 South Beverly Drive, Beverly Hills, CA 90212.

Organize a Protest

A boycott (or, in this case, a "girlcott") is a formal protest against a company whose policies or products are offensive or unfair. You might choose to boycott a company for things like promoting unsafe products or running ads that promote racism. Boycotting means not buying the company's products, telling the company why you aren't, and perhaps most important, getting other people to

Cutting Girls Down to Size

By JEAN KILBOURNE ★ Boston, Massachusetts

Advertising tells us that the way to be happy is through the consumption of material objects. Girls are told by advertisers that what is most important about them is their perfume, their clothing, their bodies, their beauty. Most of us know by now about the damage done to girls by the tyranny of the ideal image, weightism, and the obsession with thinness. But girls get other messages too that "cut them down to size" more subtly. In ad after ad, girls are urged to be "barely there"—beautiful but silent. Many ads in teen magazines feature girls and young women in very passive poses, limp, doll-like, sometimes acting like little girls, playing with dolls and wearing bows in their hair. They are shown with their mouths covered—such as when a girl is wearing a turtleneck turned up or covering her lips with her hand. These ads are selling sweaters and nail products, but they are also selling the idea that women should be silent. This may not be intentional on the part of the advertisers, but it doesn't matter; we still get the message.

In parents' magazines, boys are active and girls are passive. A boy plays on the jungle gym in one ad, while in another, a girl stands quietly, looking down and holding some flowers. Girls are often shown as playful clowns, perpetuating the attitude that girls and women are childish and cannot be taken seriously, whereas even very young men are generally portrayed as secure, powerful, and serious.

join you. If enough people do, the company is sure to feel the heat and may respond. For example, in the 1970s, activists boycotted the Nestle Corporation for promoting its infant formula in third-world countries. Activists argued that the use of formula was more dangerous than breastfeeding because the water in many third-world countries is contaminated, and mixing it with infant formula could endanger babies' lives. The boycott didn't have an effect on Nestle's sales and profits, but it did raise the company's awareness and caused the World Health Organization to set guidelines for advertising infant formula.

You can recruit people for a boycott by creating a flyer describing why you're protesting. List the company's products and include the name of its president or chief executive officer (CEO), along with the phone number for the corporate office, and what you want people to do. Then hand out the flyer at school and community events (you might even stage a boycott as a class project). You can also join an existing boycott started by a group like Mind on the Media, which identifies what needs protesting and tells you what you can do.

People in control of their lives stand upright, alert, and ready to meet the world. In contrast, females often appear off-balance, insecure, and weak. Often our body parts are bent, conveying unpreparedness, submissiveness, and appeasement. We appear psychologically removed, disoriented, defenseless, spaced out. Girls and young women are often presented as blank and fragile; floating in space, adrift in a snowstorm.

This relentless trivialization of a girl's hopes and dreams and her expectations for herself cuts to the quick of her soul. Just as she is entering womanhood, eager to spread her wings, to become truly empowered, independent—the culture moves in to cut her down to size.

What can we do as girls and women to confront these advertising images? Consciously pay attention to the ads—when we become consciously aware of their underlying messages, we reduce their power over us. We should talk with each other about how these messages make us feel. We need to educate ourselves; to read more about advertising and the media and learn how it affects us. And of course we need to talk *back* to the advertisers—sometimes privately, by ridiculing them, and sometimes more publicly, by speaking out or writing to them. Change won't come from the advertisers, it will come from citizens demanding that they change their practices.

Jean Kilbourne is an internationally recognized advertising critic and the author of Can't Buy My Love.

"Dear Company..."

Sixth-, seventh-, and eighth-grade girls in a Girl Scouts–Illinois Crossroads program called Making Choices decided they wanted to protest companies' sexist and degrading ads they found in magazines, so they formed teams and launched a letter-writing campaign. Here's what they said about the ads they chose:

Product: Lipton tea

Ad image: Woman getting a massage

Girls' response: A woman's naked body should not be used to sell your product. What does this have to do with tea? Men also drink tea—why don't you show a naked man? We would like to see a clothed, professional woman in a powerful role promoting the product. We choose not to buy Lipton tea, and we are surprised that you would stoop to this level.

Product: Buffalo shoes

Ad image: Young, scantily clad woman sitting on old man's lap in little-girl pose

Girls' response: We object to your ads showing women in sexual poses, especially the one of the young woman sitting on the old man's lap. We want to see women shown in a positive manner, standing up and projecting strong self-esteem. We want you to change your ads or we will tell our families and friends to not buy your products.

Product: Boucheron Perfume

Ad image: Nude woman from the back with her hands bound at the wrists

Girls' response: We object to your showing a naked woman with her hands tied behind her back. How about showing the product you are selling? We choose not to buy your product until you change your ads. We look forward to hearing from you.

Product: Pepe Jeans

Ad image: Couple lying on a couch; the woman looks like a mannequin

Girls' response: We don't like the way you show women in your ads in a disrespectful way. You show a man controlling a woman and a woman who doesn't seem to care what happens to her. We want to see the jeans! We also want to see all varieties of women . . . all shapes and sizes. Better role models are very important. If you don't change your ads, we won't buy your product. We also plan on telling our friends and families.

GOOD NEWS

Since 1982, the number of women working in advertising agencies has increased 45 percent, and many of them are now becoming senior executives. Women's rights advocates hope this will translate into less sexist advertising.

FOR MORE INFORMATION

About-Face, *www.aboutface.org*. Presents "galleries" of offensive and good ads, plus sample letters to advertisers and students' projects.

Can't Buy My Love: How Advertising Changes the Way We Think and Feel (Free Press, 2000), by Jean Kilbourne. The definitive guide on how advertising portrays and affects women and girls. Visit Jean's web site, *www.jeankilbourne.com*.

Sticker Sisters, *www.stickersisters.com*. Has stickers reading "This insults girls," which can be stuck on sexist ads.

Also see the resources on page 81.

Chapter 14

Creative Differences

Think of a famous painter, sculptor, composer, novelist, dancer, musician, playwright, or poet. Why, there's Baryshnikov, Beethoven, Da Vinci, Dickens, Frost, Homer, Michelangelo, Monet, Shakespeare, Whitman, and Wordsworth.

Lots and lots of guys. How about a woman?

If most history books are to be believed, very few females of the same creative caliber have come along. In truth, there've been some, since talent doesn't discriminate, but as females, they've been overlooked. Some lacked opportunity because they were loaded up with domestic work and didn't have time to develop their talents. A few who showed promise *would have* had the time to hone their skills but weren't allowed the same levels of education or privileges as men. For example, in the Middle Ages and during the Renaissance, male artists were the only ones invited into the prestigious art guilds and offered the high-level training that frequently led to their success.

The one arts venue in which women historically *have* been well represented is literature, partly because they could write when they were finished with chores at home. No matter that writing was considered "unfeminine" and popular magazines and journals wouldn't take female writers seriously—many simply used male pen names (such as novelist George Eliot, who was actually Mary Ann Evans.) Fortunately, pen names are no longer needed for success. Toni Morrison, Amy Tan, Louise Erdrich, Maya Angelou, Wendy Wasserstein, J. K. Rowling, Alice

Walker, Ann Lamot, and Candice Bushnell are just a few writers who've been penning award-winning, bestselling stories, novels, plays, screenplays, and TV series.

How do women artists in other areas rate today as compared with centuries ago? *Much* better, according to the Guerilla Girls, a cool activist group that's been working for twenty years to give women in the arts their due (see pages 110–111). However, they report, it takes time to turn around age-old favoritism of men: "In museums, major collections, and auctions sales, things are still pretty dismal for all but white guys."

THINGS TO DO ————————

Develop Your Talent

Do *you* have a creative message for the world—either expressing or celebrating what it means to be female or something else? If you want to be a painter, novelist, musician, illustrator, dancer, designer, actor, producer, director, or some other type of creative person, the twenty-first century is an ideal time to go for it. Who knows—you could follow in the footsteps of photographer Annie Liebovitz, choreographer Martha Graham, artist Frida Kahlo, or actor and director Jodie Foster. Or you could end up blazing your own uniquely artistic trail.

Discover Creative Women from the Past

Wondering what subject to tackle for that next "free-choice" class assignment? How about researching and reporting on a woman in the arts? If you're an artist in the making, this is bound to inspire. Choose one person to profile or include several women from a particular era or medium. Need ideas? There are lots of new books on female artists from both the past and the present; see the list on pages 113–114 for titles you're likely to find in libraries and bookstores.

Write Your Own Fairy Tale

Rapunzel . . . Cinderella . . . Sleeping Beauty . . . these are stories kids have loved for generations. But you've no doubt noticed that the star characters don't exactly take charge. A prince has to rescue each swooning heroine.

Why not craft your own fairy tale that features *you* as the competent and capable heroine? (Perhaps there'll be a prince too, but he doesn't have to take all the credit and have all the fun!) This can be more inspiring than reading something by the Brothers Grimm, because you create and control the story. It can have any plot you want. It doesn't have to be realistic; fairy tales are typically full of magic and make-believe. The structure should go roughly like this: Faced with a difficult situation, you must find your way through it. You undertake some kind of adventure, and whether you meet up with others on the way or go it alone, whether you confront fear and enemies or breeze along, you ultimately emerge victorious.

Getting writer's block? Read some of the collections of modern folktales (see page 114) that feature girls and women as the happening heroes. These entertaining stories will help you imagine your own plot. Then fire up your computer (or get out a pencil and paper) and imagine something grand. If you could take on any challenge—real or fictional—what would it be? What bumps in the road would you face, and what rewards would you reap?

When you've finished writing, share your story with a friend (the two of you could write and swap stories). Then write another.

Paint Your Town

Organize a group of friends to design a mural (a large work conveying a particular theme) that honors girls and women. You and your friends don't have to be fantastic artists—this is more about group co-creation. When you have five or six people excited about the idea, come up with a theme (such as female contributions to society, women in leadership roles, or famous goddesses).

Ask everyone to chip in for art supplies, then buy some heavy-duty paper made for painting, acrylic paint, a few pencils for sketching the design, wide masking tape (to secure the mural while you're working on it) and paintbrushes. Convert jars into water containers. Tape the paper on a wall in someone's house or garage or in some other convenient place. Do a rough sketch and then get to work.

When you've finished, invite your family and friends to an art opening to celebrate. Then look for opportunities to display the piece (such as during the month of March, National Women's History Month, or at a local kids' art show).

Treat Your Ears to the Women's Philharmonic

The award-winning Women's Philharmonic is a nationally renowned orchestra whose goal is to bring female composers into the mainstream music world. Check out its Web site, www.womensphil.org, to order its CDs or to find out when and where it (and other women's orchestras) will be giving concerts. You can also make contact via phone, at 415-437-0123, or mail, at 44 Page St., Suite 604D, San Francisco, CA 94102-5986.

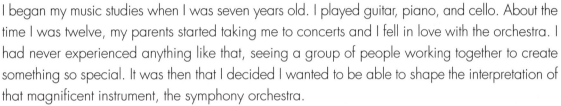

Leader of the Band

By JOANN FALLETTA ★ San Francisco, California

I began my music studies when I was seven years old. I played guitar, piano, and cello. About the time I was twelve, my parents started taking me to concerts and I fell in love with the orchestra. I had never experienced anything like that, seeing a group of people working together to create something so special. It was then that I decided I wanted to be able to shape the interpretation of that magnificent instrument, the symphony orchestra.

I first went to the conservatory when I was eighteen. I spent an entire year before I was permitted to major in conducting because the college administrators said no woman had ever succeeded in the field. They didn't want to encourage me to be a conductor because they could not see any chance of my succeeding in that exclusively male domain. It took me a year to convince them. Their resistance surprised me. I just kept doing as well as I could in my courses and telling them I was interested and that I recognized it had never been done. I was lucky when a new teacher came to the school who was a little younger and more understanding about the possibilities for women.

Today the major symphonies, particularly the older musicians and older board members, still have some reservations about a young American woman conductor. We will change that attitude through professionalism and hard work. I have three orchestras and I conduct about 120 concerts a year. I could never have predicted this ten years ago. But I always felt that somehow I would make it because I knew I wanted it so much. I had the good fortune to be invited as a guest conductor all over the United States, Europe and Asia. Of course there are disappointments and difficulties, but the moments of magic more than make up for them. To hear a Mozart symphony take shape in your hands, to see an orchestra work with all its heart and talent toward the creation of something beautiful, to feel that together we have moved and uplifted our audience beyond the cares and troubles of their everyday lives—all this makes working as a conductor the realization of my most cherished dream.

JoAnn Falletta is music director and conductor of the Virginia Symphony Orchestra and the Buffalo Philharmonic Orchestra.

Q&A with the Guerrilla Girls

Note: The group members prefer to remain anonymous, so they go by names of deceased women artists and writers.

How did the Guerrilla Girls get started?

Kathe Kollwitz: In 1985, The Museum of Modern Art in New York opened an exhibition titled *An International Survey of Painting and Sculpture*. It was supposed to be an up-to-the minute summary of the most significant contemporary art in the world. Out of 169 artists, only thirteen were women. All the artists were white, either from Europe or the U.S. That was bad enough, but the curator, Kynaston McShine, said any artist who wasn't in the show should rethink "his" career. And that really annoyed a lot of artists because obviously the guy was completely prejudiced. Women demonstrated in front of the museum with the usual placards and picket line. Some of us who attended were irritated that we didn't make any impression on passersby.

What did you do?

Frida Kahlo: We decided to find out how bad it was. After about five minutes of research we found that it was worse than we thought: the most influential galleries and museums exhibited almost no women artists. When we showed the figures around, some said it was an issue of quality, not prejudice. Others admitted there was discrimination, but considered the situation hopeless. The artists blamed the dealers, the dealers blamed the collectors, the collectors blamed the critics, and so on. We decided to embarrass each group by showing their records in public.

Do you really want to rewrite art history and cancel out all the white male artists we know and love?

Georgia O'Keeffe: Yes and no. History isn't a fixed, static thing. It always needs adjustments and revisions. The tendency to reduce the art of an era to a few "geniuses" and their masterpieces is myopic. There are many, many significant artists. We're not going to forget Rembrandt and Michelangelo. We just want to move them over to make room for the rest of us!

Why are you anonymous?

GG1: The art world is a very small place. Of course, we were afraid that if we blew the whistle on some of its most powerful people, we could kiss off our art careers. But mainly, we wanted the focus to be on the issues, not on our personalities or our own work.

Why are you Guerrillas?

Georgia O'Keeffe: We wanted to make people afraid of who we might be and where we would strike next. Besides, "guerrilla" sounds so good with "girl."

Why the gorilla masks?

Kathe Kollwitz: One story is that at an early meeting, an original girl, a bad speller, wrote *Gorilla* instead of *Guerrilla*. It was an enlightened mistake. It gave us our "mask-ulinity."

How many are you?

Lee Krasner: We don't have any idea. We secretly suspect that all women are born Guerrilla Girls. It's just a question of helping them discover it.

Have you made a difference?

Emily Carr: We've made dealers, curators, critics and collectors accountable.

Frida Kahlo: Just last year, Robert Hughes, who in the mid-eighties claimed that gender was no longer a limiting factor in the art world, reviewed a show of American art in London for *Time* and said "You don't have to be a Guerrilla Girl to know that there weren't enough women in the show."

Kathe Kollwitz: Museum curators feel compelled to suck up to us on camera. They used to ignore us and hope we'd just go away.

You sound surprised by your success. What did you expect?

Romaine Brooks: We didn't expect anything. We just wanted to have a little fun with our adversaries and to vent a little rage. But we also wanted to make feminism fashionable again, with new tactics and strategies. It was really a surprise when so many people identified with us.

Where do you go from here?

All: Back to that jungle out there. Back to work.

The Guerilla Girls have produced more than one hundred posters, stickers, books, printed projects, and actions that expose sexism and racism in politics, the art world, film and culture at large.

Character Flaws

By MARIE G. LEE ★ New York, New York

When I was in Korea for the summer, my twelve-year-old cousin fell so in love with the Disney movie *The Little Mermaid* that she bought an English-language copy of the book.

I read the book to her at least once a week. The story started to annoy me because I liked the original Brothers Grimm version better: The Little Mermaid foolishly pursues a prince and ends up turning into sea foam. In the Disney version, she ends up *marrying* the prince.

But what really began to annoy me was how all the "good" characters were male: the father, the prince, the lobster, etc. The "bad" character was the sea witch, who schemes to steal the Little Mermaid's lovely voice.

That made me think about the female characters in fairy tale movies from my own childhood. For instance, why is the villain in *Snow White* an evil, jealous mother (and the prince and the elves are all male and good)? In *101 Dalmatians*, the villain is Cruella, who wants to kill Dalmatian puppies just so she can have a fur coat to match her hair. And let's not forget *Cinderella*, with its record-breaking three evil female characters.

Almost everyone grows up seeing one if not all of the movies mentioned here, and this points out a need to look at books and movies to examine how our society portrays and regards women. Too often we are ready to accept whatever is shown to us, even when we know better. For me, it took reading this story to my cousin over and over again to see what was wrong with it. I know that as a writer I will try to include many positive female characters inspired by the *real* women—my mother, my sister, my aunt, my friends—in my life.

Marie G. Lee has written several fiction books for teens, including Finding My Voice.

FEMALE FIRST

NAME: A girls' choir at Winchester Cathedral
FIRST FEMALES TO: sing at Winchester Cathedral

This church was off limits to female choir singers for nine hundred years. Why? Many people think boys' voices are superior and worried that including girls could tarnish the choir's reputation, said the cathedral's dean. But after a girl unsuccessfully tried out for the boys' choir and mentioned taking legal action, the cathedral added a separate girls' choir. In 1999, an eighteen-member group of girls began singing there once a week.

Cool Quote

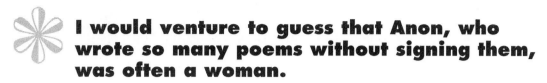 **I would venture to guess that Anon, who wrote so many poems without signing them, was often a woman.**

—VIRGINIA WOOLF, writer

FOR MORE INFORMATION

Cool Careers for Girls in Performing Arts, by Ceel Pasternak and Linda Thornburg (Impact Publications, 2000)

Create Your Own Girl Band, by Janet Hoggarth (Scholastic, 2001)

Dream/Girl Magazine, published by dgArts, P.O. Box 51867 Durham, NC 27717; *www.dgarts.com.* A magazine for girls ages 8–14 interested in arts and literature; also publishes girls' work.

Girl Director: A How-to Guide for the First-Time, Flat-Broke, Film & Video Maker, by Andrea Richards (Girl Press, 2001)

The Guerrilla Girls' Bedside Companion to the History of Western Art, by the Guerrilla Girls (Penguin USA, 1998)

Ladyslipper, 3205 Hillsborough Road in Durham, NC 27705; (800) 634-6044 or (919) 383-8773; *www.ladyslipper.org.* A nonprofit organization that distributes recorded works by women musicians, writers, performers, and composers. Free catalog.

National Museum of Women in the Arts, Education Department, 1250 New York Ave. NW, Washington, D.C. 20005; 202-783-5000; *www.nmwa.org.* Visit this museum when in Washington, D.C. Has an interactive workbook and other materials written for Girl Scouts.

BIOGRAPHIES OF WOMEN ARTISTS

Girl Groups: Piano, Vocal, Guitar, edited by Hal Leonard (Hal Leonard, 2000)

Great Women Comedians, by Gail B. Stewart (Lucent Books, 2003)

In Real Life: Six Women Photographers, by Leslie Sills, et al (Holiday House, 2000)

Making Waves: 50 Greatest Women in Radio and Television, by American Women in Radio and Television (Andrews McMeel, 2001)

More Spice Than Sugar, by Lillian Morrison (Houghton Mifflin, 2001)

Women Artists, by Margaret Barlow (Beaux Arts Editions, 2001)

Women Artists: An Illustrated History, by Nancy G. Heller (Abbeville Press, 1997)

Women Writers, by Rebecca Hazel (Abbeville Press, 2002)

"Women of Achievement" series (Chelsea House)

FOLKTALES AND STORY COLLECTIONS

Fearless Girls, Wise Women, and Beloved Sisters, edited by Kathleen Ragan (W.W. Norton, 2000)

Girls to the Rescue (series), edited by Bruce Lansky (Meadowbrook).

The Maid of the North: Feminist Folk Tales from Around the World and *Tatterhood and Other Tales*, edited by Ethel J. Phelps (Feminist Press, 1989; Bt Bound, 1999)

Not One Damsel in Distress: World Folktales for Strong Girls, by Jane Yolen (Silver Whistle, 2000)

The Serpent Slayer and Other Stories of Strong Women, by Trina Schart Hyman (Little, Brown, 2000)

Stay True: Short Stories for Strong Girls, by Marilyn Singer (Scholastic, 1998)

Chapter 15

Working Woman

Are you bored with the idea of "career planning"? Do you secretly hope—against all realistic expectations—that a prince will sweep you off your feet and relieve you of responsibility? Would you rather go buy cool stuff at the mall than save money?

If you answered yes to any of these questions, this chapter is especially for you. Earning your own money and using it to your advantage is guaranteed to impact your life in a big way. A fulfilling career, a self-reliant mindset, and a savings account are perhaps the three most significant investments you can make in yourself. A career you love will challenge you intellectually, give you a sense of purpose, help you learn new skills and reach new heights, and raise your self-confidence. A salary of your own lets you take care of yourself and make your own decisions. And money in the bank translates into flexibility to do whatever you want to do—such as buy a home or start a business—whenever the time is right.

Your personal success is worth taking seriously, and so is the success of working women as a group. Like other areas of society, corporate America could stand to improve in the equality department. Across the board, women need the same pay, opportunities, and advantages that men enjoy.

Heigh Ho, Heigh Ho . . .

Most American women work outside the home. This is a big change from just a few decades ago, when virtually all married women stayed home and ran the household. Back then, companies and the government could blatantly discriminate against women in hiring and promotion. Women are now a major segment of the workforce partly because of laws allowing them to work and partly for economic reasons (it used to be that a family could live on the father's income, but now, because of inflation, two incomes are generally needed).

However, work is not just a way for women to pay the bills. According to research firm Catalyst, 67 percent of working wives who have working spouses would keep right on working even if they didn't need the pay. Why? One reason is that when women contribute income to their families—as opposed to filling the undervalued role of homemaker—they feel more on equal footing with their partners; they've literally earned the right to half the decision making.

Bringing Home the Bacon

Did you know that, on the average, women earn less money than men? According to the U.S. Bureau of Labor Statistics, *a lot* less: only 78 cents for every dollar men earn (it's slightly higher for girls; one survey found that they earned 83 cents to boys' dollar). In addition, female-dominated jobs (such as receptionist and cosmetologist) pay less than male-dominated jobs with "comparable" skill levels (such as maintenance worker and electrician). Childcare is a great example. According to Business and Professional Women/USA, childcare workers—98 percent of whom are female—earn less than amusement park attendants and car washers, even though the work they do is critically important for a healthy society and requires some higher education.

In the past, men supposedly were paid more than women because they had families to support (as if women *didn't*). There's absolutely no excuse now; a large number of women are supporting or helping support families. But the bigger point is this: Even if women *don't* have families to support or they have a spouse who works, they deserve equal pay.

Hitting the "Glass Ceiling"

You've probably heard of the *glass ceiling,* which refers to an invisible barrier of discrimination that stops many women from moving up into leadership positions such as CEO and president. Men make up about 84 percent of the people running America's major companies (the corporate officers). That statistic is better than it was ten years ago, but it's still dismal.

Why is the glass ceiling so uncrackable? According to Catalyst, the main reason is women's lack of relevant general management or line experience (positions that have a path to the top). Companies are typically organized so that certain jobs, such as in public relations or human resources, aren't high enough status to be in the "pipeline" to the top. But departments such as public relations and human resources are the ones that have lots of women. Another problem is that women often find themselves left out of the informal corporate networking (buddying up to help each other) that men do, so they miss opportunities. And a third is that sexist stereotypes are still alive in many organizations.

Things aren't all bad, however. While progress may be slow, it's steady, and there are constant signs of hope. For instance, the National Association for Female Executives recently concluded, "It's getting easier for women to find companies where they can succeed."

Starting Your Own Business

One reason more women aren't swarming the glass ceiling is that corporate business doesn't appeal to huge number of females (only about 9 percent see it as their first-choice career). In addition, many women get disillusioned with corporate jobs and leave. Where do these women go? To start their own company! Almost *half* of the businesses in the United States are owned by women.

There are certainly advantages. Entrepreneurs say their lives are more personally rewarding and meaningful than when they were at another company because they're doing something they believe in and they're in charge. Self-employed people can also enjoy more flexible schedules since *they* determine when the work gets done. And there's one more little incentive: Running a business has the potential to be more profitable than working for someone else.

Doing It All

A common dilemma for women with children is how to balance a high-powered career with the demands of family life. Some moms work full-time (such as if when they're the sole provider for the family), or (if they can afford it) part-time or they're stay home moms. In the past, men didn't have to worry about how to work *and* raise a family since women were expected to handle virtually all the child care. But most working moms *do* have to worry about how to do both, and whether they'll face consequences. For example, some moms get "demoted" to the lower-level "mommy track" at work. Others put in their time at the office but then feel guilty about not devoting more attention to their kids.

Women's rights activists believe moms should have the flexibility both to do well in their jobs *and* to attend to needs at home; after all, working and raising America's next generation are both valuable pursuits. The majority of girls (60 percent in one survey) believe they'll need or want to take time off from a career to have children, and they should be able to easily do this without harming their career advancement. Fortunately, as more women join the workforce (in higher numbers than men*), family considerations are gaining clout. And companies that give parents more flexibility to manage family emergencies (such when children are sick) are winning praise and dedication from their female employees.

A parallel goal is to upgrade the status of stay-home moms, who, as *"just homemakers"* are essentially invisible. Most homemakers work as hard as (or harder than) those who go to the office, yet they receive neither a paycheck nor much credit. In a truly pro-female society (such as in Switzerland), people caring for children are highly valued and working moms are fully supported with excellent day care, health insurance, and the flexibility to take time off from work. American women deserve the same!

THINGS TO DO

Explore Your Career Options

Maybe you've always known that you want to be a nuclear physicist or a famous designer. Or maybe you have no idea what your future holds. Either way, the exercise on page 119 will help you discover what jobs and careers might be good fits for you.

Set Up Informational Interviews

One way to collect ideas about careers is to ask women (and men, if you like) to tell you about their jobs. This is called informational interviewing. If a specific job interests you, ask your family and friends if they know someone in that field. If they don't, ask for names of others you could ask. When you find a willing interviewee, plan to talk for fifteen minutes at most (since people are busy). Here are good questions to ask each person:

---

*Catalyst projects that by 2010, the number of working American women will have grown by almost 10 million—a rate *almost a third higher* than that of men.

1. What's your typical day like?

2. What skills do you use on the job?

3. How did you start doing this?

4. What do you like most and least about your job?

5. What obstacles have you encountered?

6. Are you interested in changing careers? Why or why not?

7. Are women in your profession treated the same way as men?

8. If you could live your career life over again, what would you do differently?

9. Do you have any advice for me?

After each interview, send a short thank-you note (postal mail is more personal than e-mail) letting the person know you appreciated the interview and mentioning something you learned. Then set up an interview with someone else. The more interviews you do, the more complete you'll make your careers "database."

What's Your Dream Job?

You'll need a few sheets of paper for this exercise.

1. Think of three things you've done that you're proud of. They can be big things—such as winning a contest or creating a thing of beauty—or small things, such as organizing a group activity, making a presentation, or doing volunteer work for Earth Day.

2. Write a detailed account of how you did each of these things.

3. List all the skills you used for each task. Include anything you did to get the job done, including such activities as writing, repairing, drawing, explaining, planning, designing, researching, analyzing, building, contacting people, working on a computer, listening, and getting people's opinions.

4. Compare your three lists. Are any skills on more than one list? Circle these common skills—they're the ones to examine more closely.

5. Sit down with a parent, mentor, or counselor (if your school has one) and discuss how you could use skills in a career. Brainstorm five possible careers and rank them according to your interest level.

6. Find out more about these careers (check out some of the resources at the end of this chapter).

7. From time to time, go back and review your list. Have your interests changed?

—Adapted from What Color is Your Parachute? by R. Nelson Bolles

Be CEO for a Day

Another way to expand your career knowledge is to go to work with a woman who has a job that intrigues you, whether it's in construction or computer software. The ideal time to do this is Take Our Daughters and Sons to Work Day, the fourth Thursday in April. Visit the event's Web site, www.daughtersandsonstowork.org, for tips on planning what you'll do.

Try Your Hand at Leadership

According to a study called "Teen Girls on Business," girls who think of business as their first-choice career often belong to clubs, teams, or social organizations where they play leading roles; they're also more likely to hold jobs than other girls. If you're curious about how the business world works, get your feet wet by joining a club and taking responsibility for a project. This could be a deciding factor in whether you choose to pursue a business career.

Become an Entrepreneur

Being your own boss, running your own show, calling the shots. More and more teens are thinking about starting their own businesses someday . . . or today. Are you one of them? If you might be, think of an idea for a business (if it stems from your interests or hobbies, that's ideal). Enter the concept in the National Business Plan Competition for Teen Women (see page 124). Contest winners receive a free trip (locations vary) and a business resource kit, and they get to meet women business owners. Past winners have started a soccer camp for younger girls, a mail-order clothing company for tall girls, and a service that assigns odd jobs for the elderly to teen volunteers, among others. Even if you don't win, you'll learn *a lot* about starting a business.

Dust Off Your Piggy Bank

"Money is a tool for achieving and maintaining independence," stresses Joline Godfrey, the founder of Independent Means, an organization devoted to helping girls take charge of their financial lives. If you're already saving money, great! You're on your way to a more secure future. If not, it's never too late to start. Yes, you may have to cut back on clothes and makeup, but the rewards later on will be worth it. Let's say you start saving $75 a week for six months. In five years, that amount in a savings account earning 6 percent interest compounded monthly will become $4,417. Not bad for a purchase such as college textbooks or part of a down payment on your own home.

Ask for More Money

Saving money is easier when you have a few extra dollars to put away. If you don't think you're earning enough at your summer job, for example, ask for a raise. Women are less likely than men to ask for raises and promotions because they often have lower self-worth and don't want to rock the boat. Keep this in mind the next time a boss wants to give you more responsibility without higher pay: you should be compensated. It can't hurt to ask . . . and you may be surprised by how often you'll get a positive answer.

Designing a Future

By LAURA HUOBER ★ Los Angeles, California

When I was in ninth grade, I decided I wanted to start my own fashion design business. I was good at drawing outfits, and I longed to see them come to life as real clothes.

I used my after-school time very effectively to sell and produce the designs. My mother helped me find creative ways to fund the production. She suggested that I sell sketches with fabric samples to friends and then make the items to fit each person.

Once I got commitments from eight clients (after about four months), I bought all the material I needed and set out to find good tailors and patternmakers. I found most of them through connections I'd made with people in the fashion industry through internships and my mother's contacts.

During the production process, I learned more than I ever could have through classes on fashion design—not just about design but about selling, keeping my word, being precise, thinking things through, never assuming, treating my workers with respect, and communicating with others. I also learned to set budgets for each part of production, such as material, pattern making, and sewing, and not to go over them. On many designs I ended up spending more than I took in, and this taught me a lot about pricing and finding the right market.

The tricky part about doing custom-fit pieces was that the measurements had to be perfect. I planned to have the clients model the items in a mini fashion show, but a few of them didn't live nearby so I couldn't do fittings. As I feared, some of the outfits didn't fit perfectly so we had to pin them. But the audience didn't notice—they loved the show!

Now I've started selling new designs and looked into expanding my production. Eventually I want to open my own boutiques and give every woman the chance to model my creations.

You can see Laura's designs on her Web site, Lola Mode, www.lolamode.com

Postpone Starting a Family

Planning to have children? You'll help your career by waiting until you graduate from college (or several years beyond high school, if you're not going further). If you get pregnant as a teen, you seriously limit your ability to continue your education and get a high-paying job. "Between the ages of fourteen and twenty, you make critical decisions that can affect the course of your whole life—decisions about what classes to take, career options, lifetime mates, and family timing," says Betty Shepperd of Women Helping Girls With Choices. You should be able to make the best choices for your future without the interference of prematurely being a parent.

All in a Day's Work

By JASMINE J. VICTORIA, thirteen ★ New York, New York

It all started when I met news anchor Carol Jenkins at a town hall meeting for girls to inform people about Take Our Daughters to Work Day.* I was covering the event as a reporter for *Children's Express*, a children's news writing service. I asked Carol what her plans were for the day, then mustered up the courage to ask if I could spend the day with her. I was so excited when she said yes.

Several girls came to the news station that day. We were given a tour and met many other reporters, producers, and camerapeople. We got to see what goes on behind the scenes and all the hard work that goes into putting together the evening news. I learned a lot about the journalism world and specifically about the important jobs women hold.

At the end of the day, Carol asked us if anyone wanted to do a "stand-up." (This is when you stand in front of the camera and give a brief recap of the story). Everyone else was too shy, so I volunteered. I was a little nervous because it was my first time. I wasn't sure if I should act like a real reporter and say, "From Channel 4 News, this is Jasmine Victoria." I gestured over to Carol, asking if it was okay that I'd said that, and she nodded. I thought I had messed up, but at the station they liked it and did not edit out my mistake. All my friends saw me on TV and thought it was funny.

Spending the day with an important woman like Carol Jenkins, who treated me like I was special, made me realize that girls should demand more respect in this world. I'm doing that now!

*Now called Take Our Daughters and Sons to Work Day

GOOD NEWS

When seventeen-year-old Susan Sparrow of Utah found out that women in her state earned just 66 cents for each dollar earned by men, she was disappointed. So she gathered nineteen people to propose a bill to study the salary discrepancies of state employees. Even though others had tried this twice earlier and failed, her group pushed forward . . . until the Utah State Legislature authorized the study in 2003.

Hot Jobs

According to the U.S. Department of Labor Women's Bureau, when this book went to press, these were the highest-paying, fastest-growing jobs:

Biological scientist	Registered nurse
College teacher	Respiratory therapist
Computer engineer	Social worker
Financial sales agent	Speech therapist
Physician assistant	Systems analyst

Cool Quotes

The glass ceiling gets more pliable when you turn up the heat!

—PAULINE R. KEZER, politician

You know you are on the road to success if you would do your job and not be paid.

—OPRAH WINFREY, TV talk-show host

FOR MORE INFORMATION

Consumer Jungle, www.consumerjungle.org. Interactive games that make it fun to learn about being financially saavy.

Cool Careers for Girls series, by Ceel Pasternak ((Impact Publications). An in-depth look at careers ranging from construction to health care.

Cool Women, Hot Jobs: And How You Can Go for It, Too! by Tina Schwager and Michelle Schuerger (Free Spirit, 2002). Women share the details of their out-of-the ordinary jobs and careers.

Girls and Young Women Entrepreneurs: True Stories About Starting and Running a Business Plus How You Can Do It Yourself, by Frances A. Karnes, Suzanne M. Bean, and Elizabeth Verdick (Free Spirit, 1997). Girls' stories about running their own companies.

Independent Means, 126 E. Haley St., #A16, Santa Barbara, CA 93101; 805-965-0475, www.dollardiva.com. In addition to the National Business Plan Competition for Teen Women, sponsors summer programs for high-school girls.

"Money Sense: A Guide for Girls," published by the National Coalition of Girls' Schools, 57 Main St., Concord, MA 01742; 978-287-4485, www.ncgs.org.

Role Model Project for Girls, www.womenswork.org/girls/careers.html. Visit this site to read firsthand accounts of what women do in their jobs.

See Jane Win for Girls, by Sylvia Rimm (Free Spirit, 2003). Lots of research-based practical tips.

Y&E: The Magazine for Teen Entrepreneurs, ye.entreworld.org. Articles, quizzes, and ideas to bend your brain.

Conclusion

Putting This Book's Principles Into Action

Congratulations, you've finished *The Girls' Guide to Life!*

Now you know all the basics about sexism, plus what you can do about it, both in your own life and as an activist. You're ready to begin putting this book's ideas into action.

At this point, you may be revved up and ready to pass along what you've learned to anyone who'll listen. You go, girl! Just keep in mind these tips:

Be Prepared for Different Opinions

You'll find that the concept of feminism evokes a wide range of reactions from people, even among feminists. While lots of girls and women, as well as boys and men, will agree with you, others will smirk. Some boys will say that girls aren't as athletic as boys, even if girls are beating them. Some women will deny that they're feminists even as they support everything that *is* feminism. And some of your friends won't always agree with you, even if your opinion makes perfect sense and you explain it three different ways. People have their own personal convictions. Should any of this stop you from supporting and speaking out for women's equality? Not for a minute.

Respect Others' Views

No two people think alike, even among activists fighting for the same cause. For instance, some feminists feel that men shouldn't open doors for women because it implies that women need assistance. Others believe opening a door is a polite gesture to offer *anyone*, male or female. No matter how backward someone else's belief seems to you, try to "get in their shoes" and understand their thinking. Don't get on a soapbox, tell people they're wrong, put pressure on them, or put them down; they're entitled to their opinions. Instead, the best way to start a dialogue is to share how *you* feel.

Seek Out Pro-Rights Guys

The concept of girls being brainy, influential, and powerful still feels threatening to some guys, so they may steer clear of you and go toward girls who don't seem particularly brilliant or don't talk about women's rights. If you're drawn to one of these guys, don't despair; there are many other cool ones who do embrace feminist beliefs and will be "on the same page" as you. And if you're reading this book, those are the guys you're going to be happiest with in the long run.

Laugh!

The issues in this book are downright serious at times, but that doesn't mean you can't use a light touch. If you can laugh and/or make others laugh about an issue (when it's appropriate), you'll put them at ease and have more success conveying your message.

Support Other Girls

As author Robin Morgan says, "Sisterhood is powerful"—female unity is definitely one key to achieving women's rights goals. But sometimes girls can be each other's worst enemies. Instead of viewing other girls with a critical eye (which our society seems to encourage), think of them as your allies and teammates. Even if a girl is the class scapegoat, in a different clique, or has totally different beliefs than you, try to give her a break.

Be Patient

If you make an effort to stop some form of sexism in your life or in the world, you may not see quick results. Change takes time—sometimes months or years—as each generation slightly changes the status quo and society's expectations adjust. As Morgan acknowledges in *Sisterhood is Forever*, sisterhood is also "complex, hilarious, stubborn, elastic, tender, furious, sophisticated, dynamic, a work in progress." Celebrate your victories from small to large and don't give up.

Dream On

Want to achieve a noble goal for yourself or womankind? Set your sights high, and then ratchet them up a notch. Don't stop at what seems reasonable; imagine the very most amazing outcome possible. As Gloria Steinem says, "Dreaming, after all, is a form of planning." Let your mind run wild, and then get started turning your ideas into reality.

Pass This Book Around

Instead of putting it on your bookshelf, let it circulate!

Have a question or comment about something in *The Girls' Guide to Life?* I'd love to hear from you. Please e-mail me at cate@empowergirls.com (my Web site is www.empowergirls.com), or send me regular mail at P.O. Box 1964, Orangevale, CA 95662.

Catherine Dee

Cool Quote

 My idea of feminism is self-determination, and it's very open-ended; every woman has the right to become herself and do whatever she needs to do.

—ANI DiFRANCO, singer-songwriter

Resources for Parents, Teachers, and Group Leaders

If you have a daughter or you teach female students in the nine- to fifteen-year-old age range, you're undoubtedly aware of the impact that gender bias has on girls. Maybe you've wished there were some basic educational materials you could give girls to help them understand it. This book is not an exhaustive guide to every issue, and it doesn't cover topics that are more suited to older girls and young women, or that other books already cover (such as health, sexuality, and general adolescent concerns). It explains women's issues to girls in an upbeat way so they can constructively respond to challenges they face in the years ahead.

Once girls begin learning about the issues, they may turn to you for additional guidance, so here's a list of books, publications, and organizations to support *you* in supporting them (also see the resources at the end of each chapter).

Let's help this generation of girls meet the challenges of being female—and takes full advantage of the joys—with confidence, courage, and conviction!

Books and Publications

The Beauty Myth: How Images of Female Beauty Are Used Against Women, by Naomi Wolf (Harperperennial Library, 2002)

Beyond Dolls & Guns: 101 Ways to Help Children Avoid Gender Bias, by Susan H. Crawford (Heinemann, 1995)

The Body Project, by Joan Jacobs Brumberg (Vintage, 1998)

Body Wars: An Activist's Guide, by Margo Maine (Gurze Books, 1999)

But I Love Him: Protecting Your Teen Daughter from Controlling, Abusive Dating Relationships, by Jill Murray (Regan, 2001)

Can't Buy My Love: How Advertising Changes the Way We Think and Feel, by Jean Kilbourne (Simon & Schuster, 1999)

Cherishing Our Daughters, by Evelyn Bassoff (EP Dutton, 1998)

Dads and Daughters: How to Inspire, Understand, and Support Your Daughter When She's Growing Up So Fast, by Joe Kelly (Broadway, 2003)

Dangerous Dating: Helping Young Women Say No to Abusive Relationships, by Patricia Riddle Gaddis (Shaw, 2000)

Does Jane Compute?, by Roberta Furger (Warner, 1998).

Everyday Ways to Raise Smart, Strong, Confident Girls: Successful Teens Tell Us What Works, by Barbara Littman (Griffin Trade, 1999)

Feminist Parenting: Struggles, Triumphs, and Comic Interludes, edited by Dena Taylor (Crossing Press, 1994)

For All Our Daughters: How Mentoring Helps Young Women and Girls Master the Art of Growing Up, by Pegine Echevarria (Chandler House, 1998)

From Barbie to Mortal Kombat: Gender and Computer Games, edited by Justine Cassell and Henry Jenkins (MIT Press, 2000)

Girl Culture, by Lauren Greenfield (Chronicle, 2002)

The Girl Pages: A Handbook of the Best Resources for Strong, Confident, Creative Girls, by Charlotte Milholland (Hyperion, 1999)

The Girls' Guide to Life Teacher's Guide, by Catherine Dee (available from Little, Brown at www.lb-kids.com, under Educator Resources or at www.empowergirls.com)

Girls Seen and Heard: 52 Life Lessons for Our Daughters, by the Ms. Foundation for Women (Putnam, 1998)

Girls Will Be Girls: Raising Confident and Courageous Daughters, by JoAnn Deak (Hyperion, 2002)

Go Girl: Raising Healthy, Confident, and Successful Girls Through Sports, by Hannah Storm (Sourcebooks Trade, 2002)

How to Encourage Girls in Math and Science, by Joan Skolnick, Carol Langbort, and Lucile Day (Dale Seymour, 1997)

How to Mother a Successful Daughter, by Nicky Marone (Three Rivers, 1999)

No More Frogs to Kiss: 99 Ways to Give Economic Power to Girls, edited by Joline Godfrey (HarperBusiness, 1995)

Odd Girl Out: The Hidden Culture of Aggression in Girls, by Rachel Simmons (Harvest, 2003)

1001 Ways to Help Your Daughter Love Her Body, by Brenda Lane Richardson (Quill, 2001)

Queen Bees and Wannabes: Helping Your Daughter Survive Cliques, Gossip, Boyfriends, and Other Realities of Adolescence, by Rosalind Wiseman (Three Rivers, 2003)

Raising Confident Girls: 100 Tips for Parents and Teachers, by Elizabeth Hartley-Brewer (Perseus, 2001)

Raising a Daughter: Parents and the Awakening of a Healthy Woman, by Jeanne Elium and Don Elium (Celestial Arts, 2003)

Raising Our Athletic Daughters, by Jean Zimmerman and Gil Reavill (Doubleday, 1998)

Reviving Ophelia: Saving the Selves of Adolescent Girls, by Mary Pipher (Ballantine, 1995)

Schoolgirls: Young Women, Self-Esteem, and the Confidence Gap, by Peggy Orenstein (Anchor, 1995)

See Jane Win and How Jane Won, by Sylvia B. Rimm, et al (Three Rivers, 2000, 2002)

Smart Girls: A New Psychology of Girls, Women, and Giftedness, by Barbara A. Kerr (Great Potential, 1997)

Strong, Smart, and Bold: Empowering Girls for Life, by Carla Fine (Harper Resource, 2002)

A Toolbox for Our Daughters: Building Strength, Confidence, and Integrity, by Annette Geffert and Diane Brown (New World Library, 2000)

200 Ways to Raise a Girl's Self-Esteem: An Indispensable Guide for Parents, Teachers, & Other Concerned Caregivers, by Will Glennon (Conari, 1999)

Magazines and Newsletters

Daughters, P.O. Box 3280, Duluth, MN 55803, 888-849-8476, www.daughters.com.

Ms. Magazine, 1600 Wilson Blvd. #801, Arlington, VA 22209, 703-522-4201, www.msmagazine.com

Organizations

American Association of University Women, 1111 16th St. NW, Washington, DC 20036, 800-326-2289, www.aauw.org

The Body Positive, 2550 9th St., Suite 204B, Berkeley, CA 94710

CyberSisters, P.O. Box 1518, Eugene, OR 97440, 541-682-7884

Dads and Daughters, 34 E. Superior St. #200, Duluth, MN 55802-9869, 218-722-3942, www.dadsanddaughters.org

Educating Jane.com, www.educatingjane.com

Feminist Majority Foundation, 1600 Wilson Blvd., Suite 801, Arlington, VA 22209, 703-522-2214, www.feminist.org

Girls in the Game, 1940 W. Irving Park Road, Chicago, IL 60613, 773-935-2401, www.girlsinthegame.org

The Girls Project, Women Make Movies, Women Make Movies, Inc., 462 Broadway, Suite 500WS, New York, New York 10013, 212-925.0606, www.wmm.com/girlsproject/about.html

Girl Scouts of the USA, 420 Fifth Ave., New York, NY; 800-478-7248, www.girlscouts.org

Girlstart, 608 W. 22nd St., Austin, TX 78705, 512-916-4775, www.girlstart.org

Girl Tech, www.girltech.com/Mentors/MN_menu_frame.html

Math/Science Network, Mills College, 5000 MacArthur Blvd., Oakland, CA 94613-1301, 510-430-2222, www.expandingyourhorizons.org

Melpomene Institute, 1010 University Ave., St. Paul, MN 55104, 612-642-1951, www.melpomene.org

Ms. Foundation for Women, 120 Wall St., 33rd Floor, New York, NY 10005, 800-676-7780, www.msfoundation.org

National Coalition of Girls' Schools, 57 Main St., Concord, MA 01742, 978-287-4485, www.ncgs.org

National Organization for Women, 733 15th St. NW, 2nd Floor, Washington, DC 20005, 202-628-8669, www.now.org

National Women's History Project, 3343 Industrial Dr., Santa Rosa, CA 95403, 707-636-2888, www.nwhp.org

New Moon, 34 E. Superior St. #200, Duluth, MN 55802; 800-381-4743, www.newmoon.org

Principle Sources

Quiz: Women's Rights

Bureau of Labor Statistics, 2002.

Gardyn, Rebecca, "Granddaughters of Feminism." American Demographics, April 2001

Peter Harris Research Group. "The 2003 *Ms.* Magazine Survey on Women, Men, and Feminism."

Timeline: Exciting Moments in Women's History

Eisler, Riane, *The Chalice and the Blade* (Harper San Francisco, 1988)
National Organization for Women

Chapter 1: Looking Out for #1

Brown, Lynn Mikel, and Carol Gilligan. *Meeting at the Crossroads.* New York: Ballantine Books, 1993.

Hyde, Janet Shibley, and Kristen Kling, University of Wisconsin-Madison, 1999

Pipher, Mary. *Reviving Ophelia: Saving the Selves of Adolescent Girls.* New York: Ballantine, 2002.

Shandler, Sara. *Ophelia Speaks: Adolescent Girls Write About Their Search for Self.* New York: HarperPerennial, 1999.

Steinem, Gloria. *Revolution from Within: A Book of Self-Esteem.* Boston: Little, Brown, 1993.

Chapter 2: Go Figure

Brown, Catrina, and Karin Jasper, editors. *Consuming Passions: Feminist Approaches to Weight Preoccupation and Eating Disorders.* Toronto: Second Story Press, 1993.

Brumberg, Joan Jacobs. *Fasting Girls: The History of Anorexia Nervosa.* New York: Vintage, 2000)

"Eating Disorders," June 2, 2003, kidshealth.org.

Hatfield, Elaine, and Susan Sprecher. *Mirror, Mirror: The Importance of Looks in Everyday Life.* Albany: State University of New York Press, 1986.

Johnson, Norine G., Michael C Roberts, and Judith Worell. *Beyond Appearance: A New Look at Adolescent Girls.* Washington, D.C.: American Psychological Association, 1999.

Wolf, Naomi. *The Beauty Myth: How Images of Beauty Are Used Against Women.* New York: Perennial, 2002.

Chapter 3: You Go, Girl!

King, Laurel. *A Whistling Woman Is Up to No Good: Finding Your Wild Woman.* Berkeley, Calif.: Celestial Arts, 1993.

Chapter 4: Good Housekeeping

Drusine, Helen. "Just a Housewife?!" In *Sisterhood Is Forever,* by Robin Morgan, 2003

Gager, Constance T. *Journal of Marriage and the Family* (November 1999)

Hochschild, Arlie, with Anne Machung. *The Second Shift: Working Parents and the Revolution at Home.* New York: Penguin, 2003.

Mainardi, Pat. "The Politics of Housework," in *Sisterhood Is Powerful,* by Robin Morgan. New York: Random House, 1970.

Sayer, Liana. "Gender, Time, and Inequality: Trends in Women's and Men's Paid Work, Unpaid Work, and Free Time." Unpublished manuscript, Population Studies Center, University of Pennsylvania, 2002.

Working Mother, October 2001

Chapter 5: Take That!

"Dating Violence Against Adolescent Girls and Associated Substance Use, Unhealthy Weight Control, Sexual Risk Behavior, Pregnancy, and Suicidality." *Journal of the American Medical Association,* August 2001; 286: 572–579.

Levy, Barrie. *In Love & In Danger: A Teen's Guide to Breaking Free of Abusive Relationships.* Seattle: Seal Press, 1992.

National Crime Prevention Council

Silverman, Jay G.; Anita Raj, Lorelei A. Mucci, and Jeanne E. Hathaway (2001):

Ullman, S.E. (1998). "Does Offender Violence Escalate When Rape Victims Fight Back?" *Journal of Interpersonal Violence,* 13, 179-192.

Ullman, S.E. (1997). "Review and Critique of Empirical Studies of Rape Avoidance." *Criminal Justice and Behavior,* 24, 177-204

Woolley, Robert J. "Guns Effective Defense Against Rape," *Minnesota Daily Online* (February 20, 2001)

Chapter 6: Class Acts

National Coalition for Women and Girls in Education. "Title IX at 30: Report Card on Gender Equity." June 2002.

Sadker, Myra and David. *Failing at Fairness: How America's Schools Cheat Girls.* New York: Scribner, 1995.

United States Department of Education. National Center for Education Statistics (2000). "Trends in Educational Equity for Girls and Women."

Chapter 7: Math Myths and Science Fiction

"The Gender Gap: Boys Lagging." A *60 Minutes* Special Report (May 25, 2003)

Girls Incorporated. Fact Sheet: "Girls and Science and Math," 2000.

Groppe, Laura, "Girls and Gaming: Gender and Video Game Marketing." *Children Now,* 2000.

Guerrilla Girls, "The Dish on Discrimination Fall 2003," www.guerillagirls.com.

Hughes, Donna M. "Changing a Masculinist Culture: Women in Science, Engineering, and Technology." In *Sisterhood Is Forever,* by Robin Morgan, 2003

Kafai, Yasmin, with National Commission on Gender, Technology and Teaching, 1999, "Tech-Savvy Girls: Educating Girls in the Computer Age" (American Association of University Women, 2000).

"Kicking Barbie's Butt: Lecture on Women in Video Games Underlines Inequality," by Anna Kaplan, *The Retriever* (October 31, 2000).

National Center for Education Statistics, *Trends in Educational Equity of Girls & Women,* 2000

National Coalition for Women and Girls in Education. "Title IX at 30: Report Card on Gender Equity." June 2002.

Chapter 8: Leave Me Alone!

American Association for University Women Educational Foundation. "Hostile Hallways: Bullying, Teasing, and Sexual Harassment in School." 2001.

Feminist Daily News Wire, "Supreme Court: Schools Liable for Sexual Harassment Among Students," (May 25, 1999) from *New York Times*, May 25, 1999.

Harris Interactive. *Hostile Hallways: Bullying, Teasing, and Sexual Harassment in School.* 2001

Hill, Anita. "The Nature of the Beast: Sexual Harassment." In *Sisterhood Is Forever*, by Robin Morgan, 2003

National Coalition for Women and Girls in Education. "Title IX at 30: Report Card on Gender Equity." June 2002.

Strauss, Susan. *Sexual Harassment and Teens: A Program for Positive Change.* Minneapolis: Free Spirit, 1992.

Chapter 9: Know the Score

American Association of University Women. Fact Sheet: "Equity in School Athletics." January 2003.

Findlen, Barbara. "Women in Sports: What's the Score?" and Jenkins, Carol. "Standing By: Women in Broadcast Media." In *Sisterhood Is Forever*, by Robin Morgan, 2003

Girls Incorporated. Fact Sheets: "Girls and Sports," 2002; "Girls and Their Bodies," 2001.

"Interesting Findings From the Research," www.seejanewin.com/findings.htm, from research by Dr. Sylvia Rimm for See Jane Win, 2001.

"Many Successful Women also Athletic", *USA Today* (March 26, 2002), citing study by Oppenheimer.

"Title IX at 30," National Coalition for Women and Girls in Education, June 2002

"2000 High School Athletics Participation Survey," National Federation of State High School Associations, 2001.

"Women's Participation in Sydney Olympics at an All Time High," *Feminist Daily News Wire* (June 15, 2000), from Infobeat News, June 15, 2000.

Chapter 10: Media Darling

About-Face, www.about-face.org

"Children & the Media: Reflections of Girls in the Media". Children Now, 1997.

Girl Power!, www.girlpower.gov

Girls Incorporated. Fact Sheet: "Girls and Media," 2002

Girls, Women + Media Project, www.mediaandwomen.org

Media Awareness Network, www.media-awareness.ca

"Media Report to Women," fall 2003, vol. 31, number 4

Lauze, Martha M. "Boxed in: Women on screen and behind the scenes in the 2000-2001 prime-time season," 2001.

Steinem, Gloria. "The Media and The Movement: A User's Guide." In *Sisterhood Is Forever,* by Robin Morgan, 2003

Teen Health and the Media, depts.washington.edu/thmedia

Chapter 11: The "Old Boys' Club"

Catalyst. "Women in Government Fact Sheet." 2005.

"GenderGap In Government." *GenderGap,* GenderGap.com.

"Girls Hit the Political Scene: Not Only to Be Seen but Heard." *Girls Inc.,* www.girlsinc.org, May 14, 2001.

Henry, Sherrye, "Why Women Don't Vote for Women and Why They Should." *Working Woman* 19 (June 1994): 49–52, 86.

"Presidential Politics: What Girls Say!" and "Pipeline to the Future: Young Women and Political Leadership," 2000, *Girls' Pipeline to Power,* www.girlspipeline.org, site created by Patriots' Trail Girl Scout Council

Schroeder, Patricia. "Running for Our Lives: Electoral Politics." In *Sisterhood Is Forever,* by Robin Morgan, 2003

Wilson, Marie, *Closing the Leadership Gap: Why Women Can and Must Help Run the World* (Viking, 2004)

"Women in Elected Office 2004 Fact Sheet Summaries." Center for the American Woman and Politics, Rutgers, The State University of New Jersey.

Chapter 12: Spread the Word

Bem S.L. and Bem D.J. 1973. "Does sex-biased job advertising 'aid and abet' sex discrimination?" *Journal of Applied Psychology,* 3, 6–18.

Cronin & Jreisat, cited in Parks, J.B., Robertson, M.A. "Influence of Age, Gender, and Context on Attitudes Toward Sexist/Non-sexist Language."

Miller, Casey, and Kate Swift. *The Handbook of Nonsexist Writing, XX*: iUniverse.com, 2001.

Popovic, Neil A. F. "The Game of the Name." *Ms.* 5 (November/December 1994): 96.

Chapter 13: Selling Us Short

Kilbourne, *Jean, Can't Buy My Love: How Advertising Changes the Way We Think and Feel* (Free Press, 2000).

"Media Report to Women," Summer 1995

"Offensive Ads." *USA Today*, September 15, 2003

The Guerrilla Girls, "The Dish on Discrimination," www.guerillagirls.com/hotflashes/index.shtml

Chapter 14: Creative Differences

Broude, Norma, and Mary D. Garrard. *The Power of Feminist Art: The American Movement of the 1970s, History and Impact.* New York: Harry N. Abrams, 1996.

"Choir Girls Make History at U.K.'s Winchester Cathedral." *Feminist Daily News Wire,* May 17, 1999.

The Guerilla Girls. *The Guerilla Girls Bedside Companion to the History of Western Art.* New York: Penguin USA, 1998.

Chapter 15: Working Woman

American Association of University Women. Fact Sheets: "Pay Equity: Fact or Fiction?" 2001, and "Women at Work," 2003.

Bravo, Ellen. "The Clerical Proletariat." In *Sisterhood Is Forever,* by Robin Morgan, 2003

Girls Incorporated. Fact sheet: "Girls and Careers, " 2003, "Girls and Economic Literacy," 2001.

Gutner, Toddi. "The Rose-Colored Glass Ceiling." *BusinessWeek*, September 2, 2002.

"Highlights of Women's Earnings in 2001." Report 960. Bureau of Labor Statistics, U.S. Department of Labor, 2002.

"Hot Jobs for the 21st Century." Women's Bureau, U.S Department of Labor, 2000.

Leonhardt, David. "Wage Gap Between Men and Women Shrinks." *New York Times,* February 17, 2002.

"New Clues to the Pay and Leadership Gap," *BusinessWeek,* October 27, 2003. "Teen Girls on Business: Are They Being Empowered?" Simmons School of Management, 2002.

"Two Careers, One Marriage: Making It Work in the Workplace," "Women in U.S. Corporate Leadership: 2003," and "2003 Catalyst Census of Women Board Directors," *Catalyst,* 2003.

Copyright Acknowledgments

When Catherine was eight, she announced to her mom that she wanted to write books for girls. Her dream stuck, and she eventually wrote *The Girls' Guide to Life*, an effort to provide girls with all the information that she'd needed when she was growing up. The first edition became a *San Francisco Chronicle* bestseller and spawned a series of inspirational little books that includes the *Girls' Book of Wisdom* (ALA Quick Pick and Popular Paperback, *Disney Adventures* Best Book), *The Girls' Book of Friendship*, *The Girls' Book of Love*, and *The Girls' Book of Success*.

Catherine lives in Orangeville, California (near Sacramento), with her husband, Jonathan. Besides writing books for girls (and working as a marketing copywriter), she enjoys speaking to groups about girls and the issues they face.

For reviews of the books, tips for parents and teachers, quotes for girls, and recommended resources, visit Catherine's Web site, Empowering Books for Girls, *www.empowergirls.com*.

Index

Page numbers of illustrations appear in italics.